MEMORABLE DINNERS

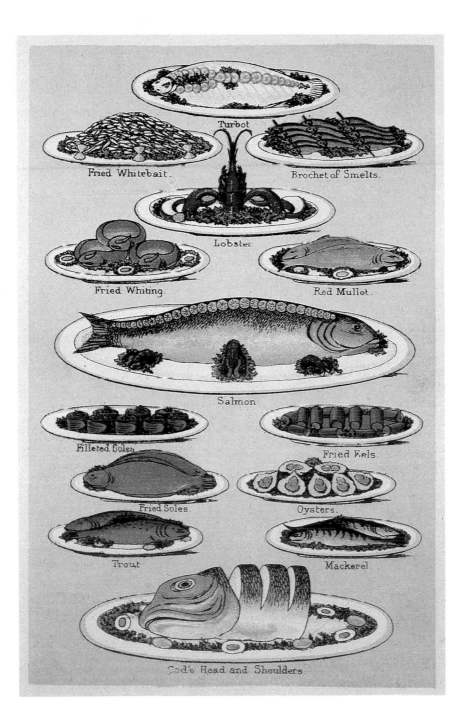

MEMORABLE DINNERS

Portentous ■ Outrageous ■ Exuberant
RECOLLECTED BY THE RICH AND RARE

Edited by DEREK NIMMO

Foreword by HRH the Duke of Gloucester

QUILLER PRESS
LONDON

Published in aid of the Order of St John

Half-title:

A plate showing fish dishes from the most famous – and successful – English cookery book ever published, Mrs Beeton's Book of Household Management. *Born Isabella Mary Mayson in 1836, she was educated in Heidelberg and trained, originally, as a pianist. She married Mr Beeton, a publisher, and began writing on cookery and other domestic matters in his* English Gentlewoman's Domestic Magazine; *it was in that journal that her famous book first appeared between 1859 and 1860. It was published in book form in 1861 and has never been out of print. Servants were, of course, an important part of any Victorian establishment above the level of the lower-middle classes – indeed, they were very much a feature of British life until the Second World War – and Mrs Beeton's book has much to say about how servants should arrange affairs for their employers. Quite how Mrs Beeton came to know so much about almost every aspect of running a household is something of a wonder, for she died in 1865, aged 29.*

Frontispiece:

French chefs, some of whom fled to England during the Revolution, gradually established their supremacy at the best hotels and restaurants. Alexis Soyer, who ran the kitchens of the Reform Club, came to London after the 1830 Revolution. But the food at men's clubs was soon eclipsed by the new restaurants. Most fashionable among these was the Café Royal opened in 1867 by Daniel Nicols and his wife Célestine. The wines were superb, described by Frank Harris, a friend of Oscar Wilde, as 'the best on earth'. This picture by Orpen, painted a little after the Café's heyday in the 1890s, reveals its magnificence. Wilde himself, accompanied by Douglas, would leave the Café Royal for a champagne dinner at the Savoy, then, after the music hall, a champagne supper at Willis's. Escoffier was in charge at the Savoy, though he later moved to the Carlton. Between the wars, another French cook, Boulestin, was to be supreme in London.

First published 1991
by Quiller Press Limited
46 Lillie Road
London SW6 1TN

ISBN 1-870948-48-3

Produced by Hugh Tempest-Radford *Book Producers*
Printed in Italy by New Interlitho

KENSINGTON PALACE
LONDON W8 4PU

TELEPHONE 071-937 6374

I am delighted that so many people should want to support the work of St. John by contributing to this book. St. John's Ambulance Brigade is visible at every major sporting or public event bringing their expertise as first aiders to those places where they are most likely to be necessary. Hopefully dinner parties should not fall into this category, though I suspect that swallowed fish bones and other disasters could well benefit greatly from those who have attended a St. John first aid course; though I hope never to have to apply the 'abdominal thrust' that is the approved last resort in such eventuality!

Dinners should be a relaxed but entertaining event with a combination of ceremony, setting, good food and interesting company. I wonder how many of these stories describe the failure of one of these categories!

I hope that all who read this book will enjoy doing so and experience the pleasures or tribulations of the contributor; I expect the knowledge that it has helped a truly worthy cause gives an extra pleasure that one good thing should lead to another. I would like to congratulate those who conceived of this idea and the generosity of those who made it possible.

Richard.

H.R.H. The Duke of Gloucester, G.C.V.O.
Grand Prior
The Order of St. John

Preface

Of all the people who have contributed to this book, we realize that our role as sponsors has been by far the easiest and most pleasurable.

We have been spared that most difficult task of choosing *one* dinner (for, in the nature of our work, there are memorable dinners all round the world, as well as here at home in Jarnac) and, even harder, recounting the experience vividly in order to share it with every reader.

It has been a pleasure and a privilege to read the contributions which day by day arrived at the St John office. That they continued to do so throughout the dark days of the Gulf War and when your postmen needed sleighs to collect and deliver them is a heartening demonstration of support for the vital work undertaken by the Order of St John, which we in France so deeply admire.

Derek Nimmo has devoted himself to his task as Editor with characteristic generosity, wit and enthusiasm, cajoling contributions from so many distinguished authors and supervising the sumptuous choice of illustrations which shed light on memorable dinners through the centuries. We thank and congratulate him most warmly.

We hope you will share our enjoyment of the pages that follow, which may well prompt you to recall with pleasure or perhaps a wry smile your own most memorable dinner.

Bernard Hine

Jacques Hine

Introduction

DEREK NIMMO

Nubar Gulbenkian once said, 'the best number for a dinner party is two – myself and a damn good head waiter.' Before starting to compile this book I myself rather tended to subscribe to that theory. Certainly some of the meals that I have enjoyed most have been eaten alone with food prepared by an inspired chef, accompanied by splendid wine and immaculate service. Only then can every mouthful be savoured, each sip of wine relished and the perfection of the service amply recorded. The whole evening is 'easily remembered' without the distraction of human conversation. But is that really what a 'memorable dinner' is about? Of course not and certainly they were not the criteria which I gave to those distinguished friends of St John from around the world whom I invited to contribute to this book.

They were simply asked to recall one particular dinner above all others. Perhaps, I suggested, they had witnessed a small piece of history being made or listened to an exceptional speech. It could be the memory of a disastrous or hilarious incident; a combination of the people present, the setting and the food which made the impression, whether utterly simple or wildly extravagant. I suggested that if it were a luncheon rather than a dinner that had left the most telling memory, the rules were only there to be bent.

The invitation was sent out on December 19th and my first reply came with almost indecent celerity from Lord Weymouth. It arrived two days before Christmas – or the winter solstice as he would call it.

We didn't hesitate to twist people's arms – after all we had the resources of St John behind us. Finally, well over 100 kind people rallied to our black-and-white flag. Everybody at St John is exceedingly grateful to all our contributors. I must add my very special personal thanks to Lord Westbury of the Order of St John whose charm does work miracles and Nancy Jarratt of Hine who is miraculously charming.

Jacques and Bernard Hine have been the kindest and most encouraging of sponsors, and giving them progress reports over their hospitable table in Jarnac has certainly added to my store of memorable dinners.

Jeremy Greenwood at Quiller Press has patiently pulled together all my threads, and Peter King's zest for finding rich and rare illustrations has been unbounded.

When the contributions began to flood in there were many surprises to be found. Who would have suspected that Michel Roux's most memorable meal (even allowing for an antipodean bride) would have been three separate but succeeding courses of Queensland Mud Crab eaten at Palm Beach on the outskirts of Sydney?

My own most memorable meal in Australia was swallowed, and

I choose my words carefully, at seven thirty in the morning on a live radio breakfast programme in Adelaide. The interviewer asked if I had ever eaten 'a pie floater'. This, it appeared, was the federal dish of South Australia. When I confessed that up until that moment the pleasure of a pie floater had been denied me they informed me that my misfortune would be rectified immediately. A messenger was sent forth, soon to return with a steaming bowl of bright green pea-soup upon which floated a meat pie, in the middle of which had been applied a too generous splodge of hospital-red Rosella tomato ketchup. Never have I witnessed at any time of the day, let alone breakfast, anything so repellent. But a memorable meal it was.

We have had several kind contributors from Australia. Andrew Peacock, Sir Rupert Clarke (whose wonderful dinners during the Melbourne Cup Spring Carnival would make a book on their own) and from the incomparable Len Evans, with whom one has enjoyed totally disastrous lunches which have developed into amazing dinners.

I greatly enjoyed the contribution of David Tang from Hong Kong. Tango, as he is known, is so posh that he makes Prince Philip sound like Arthur Mullard. He has even proposed to found in the Colony a rival Club to White's to be known as Yellows. One particularly memorable evening, I was dining with him at the Hong Kong Club with an assortment of friends, including a deeply fastidious and determinedly pompous English barrister who was sounding off, as usual, about this and that. Well come to think of it about pretty well everything. Having heard more than enough, Tang lounged back in his chair, looked at him long and hard and drawled 'You know Gilbert Rodway (for that was the QC) is the sort of person who if he went to the feeding of the 5000 would complain if he didn't have a slice of lemon with his fish.'

Jean Rook's wonderful story of her memorable dinner at the Savoy reminds me of the time that I pitched up to speak at the same hostelry. I was welcomed with that hotel's customary hospitality. A glass of champagne found its way to my hand

The 'commercial' artists whose job was to increase demand for manufactured products, particularly foodstuffs, did not hold back when it came to depicting the wares of the table. Here, Mozart's famous dinner from Don Giovanni is shamelessly used by the vendors of Leibig's meat extract, a French equivalent of Bovril.

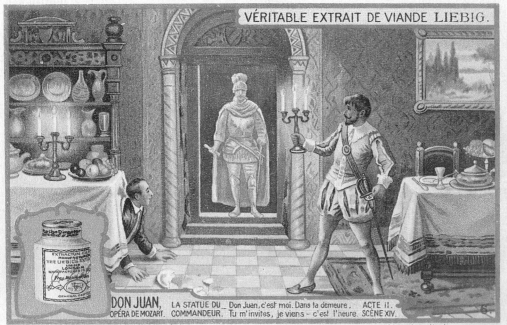

VÉRITABLE EXTRAIT DE VIANDE LIEBIG.

DON JUAN, LA STATUE DU Don Juan, c'est moi. Dans ta demeure, ACTE II.
OPÉRA DE MOZART. COMMANDEUR. Tu m'invites, je viens – c'est l'heure. SCÈNE XIV.

Voir l' explication au verso

Edward Ardizzone produced this pleasing menu for Overton's Restaurant, St James's, London, and another for the same management's restaurant at Victoria Station. More recently, David Hockney has turned his hand to illustrating the menu of a London restaurant.

Rex Whistler's menu for a farewell dinner for Professor Bernard Ashmole when he ceased to be head of the British School at Rome in June 1928.

with speed and I enjoyed several further pre-prandial tissue restorers before dinner was announced. Upon examination of the placement, however, I discovered that I was not upon it. This surprised me somewhat as I was billed to be the principal speaker. The affable maître d'hôtel, however, soon found me a table, although curiously enough it was at the back of the room. Still I had a frightfully good meal and it was only when we got to the pudding that I quizzed my neighbour about the precise aims of the charity we were both supporting. He looked at me more than nonplussed, as the dinner was being given by a company of tax accountants, not particularly known for their philanthropy. Alarmed, I looked at my ticket and was horrified to discover that I was at the wrong hotel. I should have been at the Dorchester. Heart pounding, I fled, grabbing a passing cab, and arrived deeply out of breath at the Crystal Ballroom of the Dorchester. Hardly had I settled than the gavel sounded and I was on my feet.

My conclusion from this curious episode is that the British are in general so polite and well-mannered that I suspect that one could enter ticketless, if with sufficient aplomb, most of London's major ballrooms any day of the week. There one would be welcomed, fed and wined without anyone daring to venture a question.

Sir Ranulph Fiennes reminds us of the horrors of after-dinner speaking. I particularly remember a Zontian dinner I addressed on the South Island of New Zealand. For the uninitiated, Zontians are a sort of female Mafia. I was to be introduced by Madam Chairman, who was the local headmistress. But I became increasingly alarmed during the progress of the meal by a hair which kept wafting in front of her mouth. 'When she gets up to announce me,' I thought, 'the poor darling will swallow this and choke.' So when the moment arrived when she began to address the dinner I rose with her and attempted to remove the hair with a deferential 'excuse me headmistress. . . .'

The hair turned out to be attached to a mole on her cheek and there was I, in front of 300 ladies, pulling the headmistress towards me on a long whisker. I still wake at night in a cold sweat at the recollection of the horror of it all.

From Africa Colonel Blashford-Snell tells of the strange intrusive hand which during his memorable dinner gradually worked its way up the inside of his trousers.

Having over the years collected stories of an ecclesiastical nature, I was reminded of the grand dinner at which a lady of great distinction found herself sitting next to Archbishop Trench. The Archbishop in old age lived in constant fear of paralysis. All evening he could be heard distractedly muttering to himself 'come at last; total insensibility of my right limb.' As coffee was brought the lady turned to him and said, 'Your Grace, it might be of some comfort and relief to you to know that during the whole of the meal it has been my leg that you have been pinching.'

As far as my foreword is concerned, we have certainly reached the coffee, but just before the *Hine* is served I am instructed by Lord Westbury to tell you of my own memorable dinner. It took place exactly 20 years ago and before I tell you I think it is important to explain that it happened long before I joined the Council of the World Wildlife Fund.

The dinner took place in Ton Buri on the opposite bank of the river to Bangkok in Thailand. The restaurant was named the Chokchai and it was the menu that first fired my imagination. This had a whole section devoted to wild animals, in fact it was not so much a restaurant as a zoo. You could have a 'Fried Crocodile Tail', 'Roasted Langour', 'Boar in hot chilli', 'Mountain Lizard' (that was very nice). The 'Cobra Meat' was very tasty too. The 'Tiger Meat Salad' was there if one fancied something nice and cold. If, however, you wanted the 'Elephant's Knuckle' you had to order it twenty-four hours in advance so that it could be defrosted.

Over the page was a section with a curious heading 'Misalliance Plates'. There were, apart from the obvious things like 'Fried Misalliance Pork', the rather mysteriously named 'Fried Eight Fairy' and also 'Steamed Three Fairy in earthenpot'. I didn't order that in case I was eating chums. Under the same heading you could also treat yourself to 'Rolled egg with pork and sugar pep' or the equally appetizing 'Fried Convolvulvuls' (sic). Another intriguing dish was 'Fried dried fish with holy boly holy basil leaves'.

The speciality of the restaurant, however, was bat. At the rear of the restaurant there was a large cage in which the creatures hung upside-down. You were invited to inspect the cage rather in the manner of choosing trout, crab or lobsters from a fish tank. Having selected a bat its throat was then cut and I was handed a glass of warm blood as an aperitif. A sort of bat-tail I suppose. The bat itself, which was grilled, was delicious – rather gamey and of a quite delightful texture. A totally memorable meal, but next time I think I'll just carry my bat.

Derek Nimmo
July 1991

The season, in Edwardian times, gave great scope for dinners. One variation was the dinner-dance, or dance-supper, for those young ladies who were 'coming out'. When King Edward attended, he simplified affairs by calling for champagne to be served throughout the meal instead of a different wine with each course. He also proposed having the joint of meat served immediately after the fish. Instead of the practice of placing all the plates on the table, courses were served one after another. In Mrs Beeton's words 'The table is narrow, the ladies all walk in together and are followed by the gentlemen, who sit opposite them. The servants come and hand round every dish [and] the vegetables are served in separate compartments of a large round dish.' When the gents withdrew to take port, the Prince introduced another innovation – the paper bands would be taken off their cigars in order that there could be no snobbish comparison with those who were smoking less distinguished brands than the Prince himself.

JOSS ACKLAND

Dinners We Never Had

When I decided to become a tea planter, we packed the two trunks with provisions, a duck, some chickens and a giant Indian hunting dog for protection and, together with a cook and a houseboy, set out for Likanga tea estate in Likongwe. For seventy miles we travelled rough roads until the grey-blue mysterious mountain of Mlanje came into view. The trucks bumped along uneven tracks surrounded by jungle and dense brush. A tiny wooden newly painted signpost with the words 'To the house of J. Ackland' came into view pointing along a concealed path through the jungle. Suddenly there was a clearing and in the middle stood Nachilonga bungalow. Covered with matting to keep out the sun it had a sheltered verandah which was called a *khonde* and was primitive and attractive. We quickly settled in and gradually got to know our new staff. Friday, the house-boy, had a great sense of humour, was intelligent, funny and full of gossip and was paid twelve shillings a month. There were days when his warm smile seemed more fixed than usual and he wore a tight band of wire around his forehead to cure a headache. If this failed he would cut his head with a knife to let out the blood and the pain.

'Cookie', who had four wives, was old and wise and solemn and in no time ruled the house but he was loved and respected by everyone. If Rosemary told him what we would like for dinner, he would always say, 'It is too late, Dona – I have cooked something else.'

SIR HAROLD ACTON

Memories of Railway Dinners

When I was an undergraduate at Christ Church, Oxford, in the early 1920s, a group of us used to meet together to dine at the so-called Railway Club. This was founded by John Sutro, who was omniscient about railways from their earliest days; every historical fact and he knows it – the Orient Express, the Flying Scotsman, their timetables, he has everything in his mind. And he thought how fine it would be to have dinner some-where en route!

So we would engage a whole train going to Reading or some place and dine. On the journey, we would stop at various stations for toasts, where we would be met by the station master and pose for group photographs, and there would be speeches – chiefly in honour of railway trains and the pleasure of feeling rolled off into the distance with the views   how the early trains had inspired Turner – *Rain, Steam and Speed*, an early painting of a railway train advancing, rapidly; poems on speed by Henley. It was all rather a lark, but well organized.

Once we stayed at the Royal Albion Hotel in Brighton, which was owned by a charming old man who had been a boxing expert, Sir Harry Preston. He had been much favoured and knighted by King Edward VII. He was very jolly and entertained us freely with the most wonderful meals and brandy – always with mineral water. He didn't believe in drinking brandy neat.

We had excellent dinners, very good wines. In those days, England was full of excellent wines – burgundy, claret. We would drink copiously on the journey, and arrive back in a rather sad condition. Really! Some of them. . . . Evelyn Waugh was very fond of the bottle!

LORD ALEXANDER OF WEEDON

Waiter, There's a Chicken In My Lap

The Bar Council once entertained a visiting delegation of Chinese lawyers to dinner in the fine surroundings of Middle Temple. We learned with gratitude of the Chinese tradition that after-dinner speeches should be made before dinner, so that both speakers and audience can know that the worst of the evening lies behind them. Anticipation of the dinner may sometimes shorten speeches. Our evening was so successful that the visitors invited us to enjoy their hospitality.

We were entertained in an upstairs room in a Chinese restaurant in Soho. The Chinese Ambassador was present, and proudly explained that he had taken steps to ensure that the best chefs were allocated to us for the evening. The meal was truly magnificent, and managed to avoid excesses, such as snake soup and bird's nest. But it did include the traditional lemon chicken which, after many courses and generous bibulous toasts, was placed on a dumb waiter.

At this point the former Attorney General of Hong Kong, a distinguished QC and a fellow guest, in happy and contented mood as the legal long vacation approached, raised his glass to the Ambassador and, after doing so, said 'Let me pass you the chicken.' He propelled the dumb waiter vigorously towards the Ambassador. 'Over-vigorously' might be the more accurate description, since the chicken, generously accompanied by lemon sauce, left the dumb waiter and landed slap in the Ambassador's lap.

There was momentary confusion, followed by the apologies that would be expected of courteous guests. The Ambassador trumped all this.

'My life in the diplomatic corps was serene until punctuated by re-education during the cultural revolution,' he said. 'On the peanut farms, during my period of re-training, I suffered indignities which have made me accept minor mishaps with much fortitude.' He went on to explain that, when he had presented his credentials to President Carter, he had been able to claim that they had both spent part of their lives as peanut farmers, although for very different reasons.

This response eloquently demonstrated why he had the diplomatic talents to represent his country abroad, and the evening continued in great harmony and goodwill. We were not sent a bill for cleaning the suit.

The first recorded dinner included – for dessert – the apple Eve offered to Adam. The story illustrates that man is the only animal who does not know instinctively what he should eat – he has to make a conscious choice by trial and error. Adam's diet was limited to the fruit growing in the Garden of Eden – the Bible does not suggest that he hunted for food. In contrast, post-Darwinian man's earliest ancestor, Peking Man, is known to have had a diet which consisted mainly of venison, topped up by such delicacies of the hunt as buffalo, rhinoceros and even tiger.

SIR HARDY AMIES

One Tiny Criticism

From his earliest days, man set about finding his dinner by hunting for it, with husbandry a later additional source of food. The first paintings we know that record this elemental activity were discovered on the walls of the caves of Lascaux in the Dordogne, France, by four small boys in 1940. In this picture, the hunter appears to have become the hunted and will certainly remember his dinner if he lives long enough to enjoy it. Peking Man, the cave-dweller and hunter who probably lived half a million years ago, was the first of our ancestors known to have made use of fire to improve the taste of his dinner.

On 18 December 1990, I had one of the best, if not the best, dinners I have ever eaten, given by Mrs Ulfane for the sixtieth birthday of her husband, Max. Two hundred guests were invited to dine and dance at Osterley. There was a distinguished company, placed at tables of eight. All this routine stuff – if that doesn't sound too blasé: the setting was of course splendid.

The menu was in my opinion remarkable, as you will see. Not a sign of the old caterers' clichés – Smoked Salmon, Tournados Rossini, Wiener Schnitzel, Pêche Melba.

I don't remember much about the first course: I was too busy settling myself down with my neighbouring ladies, neither of whom did I know. But I was quite alert for the main course – and keenly aware of the Margaux. The combination of lamb and fresh foie gras was quite remarkable. The service offered by the caterers was exceptionally good: a very deft staff well trained in the best traditions of a private house. Lest you should think I was quite carried away – and had my critical faculties dulled by the Margaux – I allow myself one jot of criticism: the menu was slightly let down by including the words 'Fresh Vegetables'. Of course the vegetables were fresh! A tiny thing – and not at all the fault of the hosts.

Quickly one relished a very good pudding – Christmas pudding. But remarkably served as an iced dish! I don't really like white chocolate – I think it is nasty as a sweetmeat – but as a sauce it was delicious. The herby candied taste of the pudding was most intriguing as an ice. I long for the recipe.

So we pass on over the champagne and arrive – fortuitously, but regally and correctly – at the brandy.

EVELYN ANTHONY

An Essex Dinner Party

There are some dinner parties that were such a success or such absolute disaster that they deserve a special place in the memory.

My favourite is a combination of both, and took place over twenty years ago. We had invited someone best described as the uncrowned queen of the country, who could either be an asset or a nightmare at a party, depending on her whim. On this occasion she decided to be rude and difficult and I could see the warning signs from my husband's end of the table. As it was a long table I couldn't reach out to kick the lady on the ankle.

We had a West African steward looking after us at that time. Salifu was a man of such dignity and presence that he made the grandest English butler look insignificant. He had presented the uncrowned queen with her first course, and been deliberately ignored until I hoped he'd drop it in her lap. The second course arrived. She adopted the same tactic. She behaved as if the majestic Salifu were invisible. He stood at her side and waited. The dish was poussin. I remember it so well. Succulent, beautifully presented, steaming with delicious smells. At last she helped herself from the dish without a word of thanks and went back to being the centre of attention. I made a private vow never to have her in the house again.

At the time we had an Irish wolfhound called Riley. He was a very big wolfhound, a giant with a gentle nature. He wasn't forbidden in the dining-room, or any other room in the house.

Janus feasting, from a French illumination for a fifteenth-century Book of Hours. The gods, like man, put feasting high on the agenda. Here Janus succeeds in getting two dinners for the price of one, thus disproving the adage that there is no such thing as a free dinner.

One of the most important of all the Roman deities, Janus was the god of the beginning and ending of all things — hence his name being used for the first month, January; his two faces (symbolizing the future and the past); and the two open doors in the illustration. By this date Christianity seems to have given him monks as attendants; at right is the associated sign of the Zodiac, Aquarius, the Water-Bearer.

He came in very quietly that night. I watched him pad up to the uncrowned queen. She was busy flirting with the man on her right. Riley was the most accomplished thief, able to take a leg of lamb in his jaws while your back was turned in the kitchen. He removed that poussin with the delicacy of an Artful Dodger.

I laughed. So did our other guests. The uncrowned queen wasn't terribly popular. Riley the wolfhound was licking his lips and looking angelic by the time she realized what had happened.

She had vegetables, refused the pudding and went home early. Everyone else stayed on till the small hours. They left saying it was the best dinner party they'd been to for ages. And my husband and I were convinced that Salifu had opened the dining-room door for Riley that night. He had a great affinity with dogs.

The Feast of the Gods, *probably by Marten Pepyn (1575–c. 1642), shows all divine senses fully engaged – perhaps in agreement with Shakespeare's 'I know that a woman is a dish for the gods, if the devil dress her not.'*

JEFFREY ARCHER

The Proper Use of Knowledge

In 1981 I received a telephone call from Mr Otto Preminger, who was passing through London and was keen I should join him for dinner to discuss buying the film rights for *Kane & Abel*. I explained that my wife was giving a lecture that evening and that I had been left in charge of our six-year-old son, Jamie.

'Bring him along,' said Preminger, 'I like children.'

In the car journey up to London, Jamie was full of non sequitur questions, as if I were some driving encyclopaedia. 'How high is Big Ben? How fast can this car go? How many plays did Shakespeare write? Why don't aeroplanes drop out of the sky?' I did my best to answer his questions accurately, or at least to his satisfaction.

On arrival at the Carlton Tower, Jamie was stunned into silence, as it was the first time he had been into a restaurant. This gave Mr Preminger the opportunity to tell me in great detail how he would direct *Kane & Abel*. During the second course, which seemed to keep Jamie fully occupied, I asked Mr Preminger how many films he had directed. 'Thirty-eight,' he replied.

'One more than Shakespeare wrote plays,' said Jamie without hesitation. It was to be several seconds before Mr Preminger spoke again.

On the way back to Cambridge that night, I explained to my son the meaning of the word 'precocious'.

CHRISTABEL BIELENBURG

Berlin, Christmas 1944

On 24 December 1944 I set off from Rohrbach in the Black Forest, where I was living with the children, and began the long rail journey to Berlin, where the Gestapo had given permission for me to see my German husband Peter in Ravensbrück, a concentration camp north of the city. He had been arrested after the failure of the plot against Hitler's life on 20 July that year. When I reached Berlin I hoped to find out a little more clearly how things lay; if they were as bad as I thought they might be, I would put my plan into action and ask for an interview with Peter's chief interrogator. The Gestapo apparently believed that I had very influential relations in England. I would play on that.

It was late the following afternoon and already dark when I reached our former Berlin home, now occupied by our friends Mabel and Arnold Köster, his nephew and some Dutch boys. I was hoping that Arnold would give me news of Peter, but for security reasons, we first had to go through the ritual of having dinner together, during which neither Arnold nor I could speak openly. On arrival I went to my room where I washed and tidied a bit and dug my rather meagre offerings out of my rucksack. A loaf of home-made bread, a pound of butter, a piece of smoked bacon.

Back in the sitting-room I found them all sitting round the coffee-table in front of a blazing fire – Mabel, Arnold and

If the gods, who were immortal, favoured splendid dinners, then it followed logically that in the after-life mortals would also have to look to their victuals. This wall-painting from Thebes, painted as long ago as 1400 BC, shows two rows of funeral guests waited upon by servant girls. The piles of food represented not only the earthly fare for the guests but provision for a surplus on which the owner of the funeral chamber expected to dine in his life after death.

Arnold's nephew, a fair, lanky fourteen-year-old.

They jumped to their feet when I came into the room and I sensed a slight embarrassment. I, for my part, was anxious to put them at their ease, for they were friends and I was glad of them. 'So the house is still standing, how marvellous,' I said, 'not a window broken. What do you think of my spy service? I have a special line to Bomber Harris of course, but, jokes apart, how ever have you managed it? Not a window broken as far as I can see.'

'Well, we do our best, Chris, the double windows are padded with cushions as soon as the sirens go, and there's always someone watching out for incendiary bombs.'

I placed my offerings on the table and was almost ashamed at the clamorous applause they received. 'Real bread, real butter. Oh, it's not true, and bacon – when did I last see bacon!' For some reason or other I suddenly remembered a small pot of Tiptree's Little Strawberry jam, which I had hidden in a bucket in the cellar several years ago, at the outbreak of war. 'Wait a moment,' I said, and I hustled down to the cellar stairs, past the absurd air-raid shelter equipment, and came back triumphant. 'Now,' I said, 'let's eat the lot.' It was fun watching them stuffing, especially the boy. The coffee tasted very much as it did in Rohrbach – three or four beans to a gallon of water – but it all helped a little to ease our embarrassment. The conversation had been limping along with everyone talking at once or else silence, but after the coffee it flowed smoothly enough, although always evading the main issue – the reason that I had come to Berlin at all.

When every crumb of the bread had been eaten and we were awash with coffee, and the jam pot was empty, and a huge dent had been made in the butter, Arnold gave the signal that the table should be cleared. His nephew slipped out of the room, and I heard him running upstairs to the children's room, where I supposed the Dutch boys were still camping. Mabel cleared the things, the door closed behind her and I turned instantly to Arnold, who was sitting opposite me in Peter's wing chair, staring into the fire with an odd expression on his face. . . .

'I know, I know, Chris, you can hardly wait,' he said. 'You want to hear how things stand with Peter, of course you do.'

COLONEL JOHN BLASHFORD-SNELL

Monkey Business

During the Scientific Exploration Society's expedition on the Zaire River in 1974, we had stopped our fleet of giant inflatable craft at Kindu, a small town, to prepare for the crossing of a hazardous set of rapids downriver.

While all this reorganization was going on, scientist Sinclair Dunnett and a tough Royal Marine named Bob Hudson were still pursuing the rare pygmy chimpanzee down the Lomami River, which ran parallel and to the west of the Zaire. At night we would receive faint reports from them by radio, but in spite of the most terrible privations they had not yet found the elusive creatures. With an Army Air Corps Beaver plane we supplied them by parachute, keeping our fingers crossed that nothing serious would occur, for they were well outside the range of any immediate help.

Ashurbanipal, the grand monarque of Assyria in the seventh century before Christ, at a garden banquet with his Queen, Ashursharet, possibly in the Hanging Gardens of Babylon, a city he subdued in 648 BC. Few locations can have been so magnificent for a picnic as these gardens, which were probably splendid pyramidal terraces planted on a series of ascending levels.

Cruel, luxurious and indolent, and given to trusting in omens and astrology, Ashurbanipal presided over the destruction of perhaps the greatest of all the ancient empires, which did not long survive his death in 626 BC. His legacy is a wealth of art and literature, of which he was a magnificent patron – and Kipling's lines: 'Lo, all our pomp of yesterday/ Is one with Nineveh and Tyre!' From the earliest times, food has been an essential ingredient of regal magnificence.

Belshazzar's Feast *by John Martin (1789–1854).*
'Belshazzar made a great feast to a thousand of his lords, and drank wine before the thousand. . . . In the same hour came forth fingers of a man's hand, and wrote over against the candlestick upon the plaister of the wall of the king's palace: and the king saw the part of the hand that wrote. . . . And this is the writing that was written, MENE, MENE, TEKEL, UPHARSIN.' (Daniel 5: 1; 5; 25.) Daniel the Prophet translated these words for Belshazzar, saying that God had numbered his kingdom and finished it; that he had been weighed in the balance and found wanting; and that his kingdom would be divided and given to the Medes and Persians. That same night Belshazzar was murdered.

Meanwhile in Kindu I had met the charming lady president of the local Luncheon Club, who mentioned that she also ran the cinema, night club and brothel. She invited some of my HQ staff to dine with her the next day. So, the following evening, accompanied by my assistant, Pamela, and a Zaire naval officer, I went to her house.

The lady chairman and her sister, their hair arranged in spikes and wearing traditional costume, had prepared a delightful meal of traditional Zaire dishes. We were half-way through dinner when I felt something touch my leg. It was more than that; it was quite clearly a hand which, very gradually as the meal progressed, worked its way up the inside of my trousers. Becoming slightly alarmed, I looked across to the lady opposite and was intrigued by the fact that both her hands were on the table. Eventually when the mysterious fingers had almost reached my knee I could stand it no longer and shot my arm under the table to grasp what it was. Out came a very tiny chimpanzee dressed in a sailor suit and furious at having been disturbed.

'Ah, you have found poor Sophie,' said madam.

'She must be a very young chimpanzee,' I replied.

'Ah no, she is very old,' insisted the lady.

Thus it was that whilst Sinclair and Bob were undertaking a separate and most trying expedition, I had found the extremely rare pygmy chimpanzee under a dinner-table in Kindu!

A Meal Composed of Kindness

Some friends invited me to dinner, and knowing I might be going 'vegi' once again, though I hadn't got there yet, served me some substitute chicken woven from vegetable fibres, and in the warp and woof of the phoney fowl they stuck a plastic wishbone. It was excellent, as was their seafood cocktail, composed of parsnips not prawns.

But I do not wish to mislead you. Some imitations are not that good. They look fine, and taste fine at first, but their after-taste, difficult to disguise, is the giveaway, which is why wine tasters swill their mouths out.

This is true of holy as well as profane nourishment. The same caution applies to the milk of human kindness as to the sort you consume from bottles, granules or powder. Loving words can cover a lot of looniness. Greed can be disguised as gener-osity, and just because the letter-head is religious it doesn't mean that God has dictated the contents. Taste, and see for yourself that the Lord is good, the psalmist tells us, don't rely on the promotion.

On a lecture tour, I tasted both the true and phoney forms of friendship.

At an inter-faith meeting, I sat demurely on a dais, flanked by other spiritual artistes, rather like animal turns in a humane but holy circus. The compère introduced us one by one and

Swans and peacocks were a particular delicacy at a feast, and here the birds almost distract the eye from the real subject of the painting, the head of John the Baptist being presented to Herod by Salome. The work, by the little-known Ottmar Elliger I (1633–79), was inspired by Rubens's picture on the same subject.

Sometimes a ruler would throw a dinner-party at which the guests' attention might be somewhat distracted from the food and drink. The boy-Emperor Elagabalus (Heliogabalus) ranks high in the list of insane Roman rulers, and once showered his guests with such an avalanche of sweet-smelling rose petals that a number were smothered to death; the incident is depicted here by Sir Lawrence Alma-Tadema (1836–1912). According to legend, the Emperor Nero also favoured an excess of rose petals at dinner-time.

I listened with satisfaction and surprise as he enlarged on my virtues and attainments. He singled out my sincerity, with which he claimed personal acquaintance. The introduction over, he turned towards us and said in a hoarse whisper, 'Which of you guys is this limey rabbi from England?'

But I also remember arriving at a little airport in the Midwest in winter. I was met as usual by a smiling hostess, who whisked me away happily. European rabbis were scarce in those parts and she'd got one! All the local leaders would meet me at her dinner party tonight, she told me. She had been practising French cooking for weeks, to make me feel at home. It was the summit of her social success and she sighed blissfully. When we got to her house she showed me to my room, glancing at me as she went out. She returned carrying a heavy tray. On it was a bottle of Bourbon, a bottle of ginger ale and a platter stacked with sandwiches, pecans and cookies.

'But if I eat these I won't have room for your delicious dinner,' I said, overwhelmed.

'You aren't coming to my delicious dinner,' she said flatly. 'I guess you've gone through this routine too many times, and you're tired. Have a good rest, and you'll meet folks tomorrow.'

'But what about your party?' I asked.

'They'll just have to make do with my French cooking,' she said. 'You're our guest, you come first.'

Well, the Bourbon was good but I've never forgotten the taste of that milk of human kindness, whose good aftertaste still lingers across the Atlantic. It was the real thing.

DIRK BOGARDE

A Piper to Play Us In

One of my fondest memories is of a ceremony at St Andrew's University, Scotland, where I was awarded an Honorary Degree of Letters. Why? You may well ask; it raised a few eyebrows, but I didn't give a fig about that. I was wearing a fine black satin cassock with wide cuffs. All down the front were bright yellow buttons; these designate 'The Arts'.

I was scared to death – but I survived. And in retrospect it was fun, especially the Graduation Dinner with tables at herring-bone angles and a piper to play us in. Me at the top table with silver candelabra, apricot roses, crystal and silver. Very elegant, rich apparently, established. Scowling scholastic faces in heavy gilt frames on the panelled walls, stained glass, speeches, a loving cup passed from one to another. Altogether moving, ancient and perfect.

CHRIS BONINGTON

Dinner for Two on Kongur

Life becomes very simple on a mountaineering expedition. It revolves around climbing, eating and sleeping. I find that I become obsessed with food, dream of four-course meals, of elaborate breakfasts, of crispy bacon and kidneys and Cumberland sausage and all the trimmings.

Peter Boardman, Al Rouse, Joe Tasker and I were attempting Kongur, an unclimbed peak of 7719 metres in China. We were climbing alpine-style, which entails loading your rucksack at the bottom of the mountain and keeping going until you reach the top, camping or bivouacking on the way. I was sharing a rope and tent with Joe Tasker, and we were now three long hard days out of base camp, and were feeling the debilitating effects of altitude. We had laboriously dug out a platform, pitched the tent and at last crawled into our sleeping bags, relieved at being able to stretch out and settle down for the day.

By this time we were ravenous, and later on that afternoon started cooking. Having missed one meal, even dehydrated meat balls in gravy with beans could be exciting, but I made it a little too watery and decided to thicken it with some mashed potato powder.

Al had sorted out all the food we were to take on the hill and, to reduce weight to the minimum, had thrown away as much packaging as possible, decanting the food into small plastic bags. We had little bags of milk powder, salt, sugar, lemonade powder, mashed potato powder. Unfortunately, however, we had not troubled to label them and we had packed them badly anyway, just stuffing the lot into a big bag which was now a hideous mess of loose bits of chocolate, muesli, sweets and other items of food that had escaped from their original containers.

I dug out what I thought was the mashed potato powder, licked my finger and shoved it into the powder so that I could taste some. It seemed to have a neutral kind of flavour, so, just to be sure, I asked Joe to try some as well. 'Tastes all right

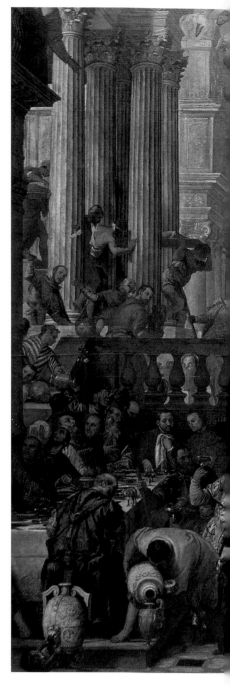

The Wedding Feast at Cana *by Paolo Veronese (1528–88). Meals figure almost as large in Christian art as they do in paintings of pagan celebrations. It was at Cana of Galilee that Christ performed His first miracle by turning water into wine when the latter had run out. The Feeding of the Five Thousand and, most notably, the Last Supper were also much favoured by the artists of the Renaissance, but Veronese*

himself fell foul of the Inquisition, which regarded his treatment of sacred subjects as being insufficiently pious. The accoutrements of the feast shown here belong not to Galilee, but to sixteenth-century Venice (note the wine coolers and other elaborate pieces of silverware), and many of the characters portrayed in this painting would have been friends or local notables.

to me,' he endorsed, and so I put the lot into the pan of bubbling mixture. It didn't thicken at all and after another few minutes I passed the pan and our sole spoon over to Joe, so that he could have the first few mouthfuls.

He took one. His expression changed from one of quiet anticipation to nausea as he lunged to the tent entrance, and spat out the entire mouthful.

'That was lemon powder you put in. Try some.' And he handed the pan over to me. It was appalling, but it was vital that we got some food down and I therefore forced down about twenty mouthfuls of the mixture before admitting defeat and pouring most of the contents away. This was the second day we had had very little to eat.

I won't forget that meal in a hurry.

Farewell Dinners

Telling someone that you don't love them after all is the hardest form of truth, particularly if you like them. If you don't give a damn then it's really quite easy, you can just be insulting and leave it at that.

One celebrated old roué from my youth used to play deliberately on his reputation whenever he wanted to disentangle himself from one doting female and get involved with another. He used to take them to the same restaurant night after night, sit them at the same table and order the same dishes every time. Why he did not arrange for the same music to be played I don't know, but perhaps he might have felt that that was going too far. After hinting darkly during the meal that something was on his mind he used to wait for the coffee before spilling the beans.

'You know how much you mean to me,' he would begin, with just a hint of regret in his voice. 'You know how much we have enjoyed being together for [and it could vary from six hours to six months]. But now we have reached a crossroads. Selfishly I wanted you to turn and come with me. But seeing you here, I realize that I have no right to ask you to sacrifice yourself to a man with a reputation such as mine. I cannot drag you down with me, my dear. I cannot ask you to waste yourself. Our love has been a beautiful thing, I cannot allow myself to taint it. We must part. You will love other men, I can tell. I will be seen with other women, I know. But they will only be substitutes for what you have meant to me.'

Then he would quickly get up and leave, overcome by emotion, before his beloved had a chance willingly to offer herself

The Bayeux Tapestry, woven in about 1080, depicts the dinner before the Battle of Hastings: William (soon to be Conqueror) banquets with Bishop Odo and his barons. To the left, one of the lesser guests is being handed what appears to be a Norman version of chicken kebab. Unseen here, further left, the servants are depicted roasting other meats over a spit. William and Odo are pictured in the act of saying Grace, despite the fact that other guests have begun to tuck in already, using their fingers. As well as the absence of knives and forks, note the use of drinking horns and bowls.

In medieval times the feast was something of a public relations exercise, with the host seeking to impress the other diners. As so often was the case, the host here is surrounded by plotters (left), hangers-on (right) and others pretending to ignore his presence. The painting, by Sir Frank Brangwyn RA (1867–1956), represents a twentieth-century view of the past.

to redeem him. Towards the end of his career he even arranged to have a taxi waiting outside to take him off to his next conquest waiting in another restaurant, out of harm's way.

Just for the record, I once had a lady friend who was just as effective in getting rid of her suitors without even having to raise the unpleasant subject of their parting. Her policy revolved around dinner, too, though this one she prepared herself. She used to serve the same meal, cream of mushroom soup, dover sole, chicken suprême and any soufflé, as long as it was white. She took care to dress entirely in white as well, and to finish the ensemble the meal was served on a plain linen table cloth, laid with plain white plates and ivory-handled cutlery. This has absolutely nothing to do with conversation of course, but the effect of all this virginal white was more than enough to quench even the most obstinate admirer's ardour.

MICHAEL BROADBENT

Fine Wines

Wine events connected with food are a main part of my life at Christie's. One I recall with mixed feelings. It was the fifth annual *Raritäten Weineprobe* organized by the indefatigable and extremely generous German collector, Hardy Rodenstock.

I flew to Düsseldorf and took a taxi to a charming country inn called Fuente, to arrive just in time for the pre-prandial glass of champagne. Forty or so guests took their places at table punctually at noon, and as the clock struck twelve midnight we arose, having had a short afternoon break – not for tea. In the meantime, we had tasted and consumed (the Germans

do not spit wine out at tastings) twelve well-placed and delectable dishes accompanied by seventy-five wines, the oldest of which was a 1727 vintage Rüdesheimer Apostelswein.

I had a terrible hangover even before the evening was out, and was horribly sick in the night. I had to get up at six to catch the eight a.m. flight from Düsseldorf back to London, flying through a terrible thunderstorm that I sincerely hoped would finish me off. At 'eleven o'clock precisely', with rather a pounding head, I mounted the rostrum to conduct our weekly auction of Fine Wines.

ANTHONY BURGESS

Two Malay Cooks

Yusof had picked up cooking in the kitchen of the Malay Regiment officers' mess, and he served us nauseating dishes with cold sculpted potatoes, parodies of some dream of the *haute cuisine anglaise*. Lynne taught him simpler recipes – stew of *kambing* (goat or mutton: one could never be sure) and even lobscouse, which was eventually adopted in the town as a dish believed to be native Malay. He would ruin these with fistfuls of caraway seeds. Eventually we lived on his curries, which, being Malay, were mild but not bad. If he stole from me, he made up for this by stealing from the store cupboards of the preparatory school mess – tinned peaches and polished rice. When he set the table he would place with the salt cellar and the Worcester sauce a tin of furniture polish. He could not read. . . .

Dinner-parties were popular venues for hatching plots. Here, the handsome but low-born Lorenzo is paying too much attention to the beautiful but high-born Isabella (who feels the same for him); her brothers, meanwhile, believing that she deserves a better class of husband, are plotting Lorenzo's end. Later, they murdered him, and buried him in a secret grave. Isabella found her beloved's last resting-place, dug him up, and cut off his head, which she hid in a pot containing a basil plant. The brothers, noticing their sister lavishing such tearful affection upon a mere herb, investigated the pot and found the luckless Lorenzo's grisly remains – overcome with remorse, they exiled themselves. Isabella, however, pined away to death. The story, which originated with Boccaccio's Decameron, was the subject for Keats's poem Isabella, or the Pot of Basil; *this 1849 painting by John Everett Millais was the first he attempted in the Pre-Raphaelite manner.*

While the medieval ruler enjoyed a good feast, he was ever conscious of the fact that one of history's lessons was that many a healthy ruler had come to grief over the dinner table owing to the treachery of his cook. Hence a constant series of vacancies for royal tasters. Here, one of the fraternity is checking the wine, and he is not concerned with its bouquet. The illustration comes from an early fourteenth-century manuscript of the Romance of the Holy Grail: *poisoned food and intrigues at banquets play an important part in the story.*

Eventually we were given a house. Mat bin Salleh (my driver) was turned into a cook, and his wife, Maimunah binte Ibrahim, into an amah. Mat became a very good cook, since he had not come to us, like Yusof, with preconceived notions of the white man's cuisine. He learned to roast a *gigot* or make a Lancashire hotpot on basic principles taught by Lynne and these to him had the remote technicality of gear changes. When we left Malaya, Mat was given a *surat* or letter of recommendation extolling his skill in the British, Indian and Italian cuisine. This he passed on to his cousin of the same name, who had no cooking skills at all, and then settled to being a royal driver.

LORD CARRINGTON

A Diplomatic Incident

In 1971, while Sir Alec Douglas-Home, the Foreign Secretary, was away, I, as Secretary for Defence, was asked to deputize for him at a dinner given by Mr Heath, the Prime Minister, for President Kaunda of Zambia. Before the dinner there had been an agreeable meeting between the Zambians and the British delegation. President Kaunda then went back to his hotel to change and returned later for the dinner.

In the interval he appeared on television declaring that the British Government's policy towards South Africa was wholly

wrong and he appealed to the British people over the heads of their government. Mr Heath happened to see this interview and took the very firm view that this was not the proper way for a Head of State, who was a guest of the Government, to behave. Had he behaved in a similar way in Zambia, there would, he thought, have been a rather volatile reaction.

Consequently, when President Kaunda arrived back at No. 10, the Prime Minister was unwilling to exert himself in any very noticeable manner. We sat down to dinner, twelve in all, to an awkward silence. I felt it necessary to try and relieve this with a series of anecdotes and stories, increasingly feeble, and all, without exception, received in total silence by everyone, including the Prime Minister. When we reached the pudding, I gave up and Sir Denis Greenhill, then Permanent Secretary at the Foreign Office, took over, with the same discouraging result.

We rose from dinner and went into the white drawing-room where, for the first time, the Prime Minister spoke. 'Mr President,' he said, 'we, over the years, have done our best to accommodate and to help the people of Zambia, yet you come to this country and seem to have no regard whatever for our interests and, furthermore, appeal to the people of this country over the heads of their Government.'

President Kaunda looked horrified. 'Never,' he said, 'did I expect to be spoken to like this by a British Prime Minister. Never, never!' – a cry vigorously taken up by the other Zambians present, relieved to be able to say something at last. Mr Heath, satisfied with his intervention, said nothing.

For the last time, and most unwisely, I spoke. 'Mr President,' I said weakly, 'the Prime Minister is trying to say that all of us have our own interests.' My voice trailed away as President Kaunda and the five other Zambians rose from their chairs and walked down the stairs and out of No. 10.

Mr Heath went to bed. Sir Denis and I had a large whisky and soda.

A Mamluk painting of an outdoor dinner-party (1337). In the East, dining customs varied less over the years than in Europe, where fashions came and went. This manuscript shows the head man (centre) making the first move by selecting a tender morsel from the communal vessel, thus signalling the commencement of the festivities. Such customs continue to this day.

DAME BARBARA CARTLAND

Melons and Gold Plates

A fifteenth-century Bruges illumination of a scene from Froissart's Chronicles. *Richard II of England (1367–1400) is shown here dining with the Dukes of York, Gloucester and Ireland, all of whom were probably dissembling about their dissatisfaction with his government. Richard was later overthrown and, according to one account, starved to death at the orders of Henry IV. Note the introduction of place settings, the elaborate silver-gilt ship used as table decoration and also the two trumpeters in the gallery.*

When I left school, one of the first big dinner parties I went to was at Arlington House, given by the fabulously rich Lady Michelham.

About thirty people sat down at a huge table covered in orchids and set with gold plates. I had never even seen gold plates before, let alone eaten off them!

The first course was a slice of Canteloupe melon and I picked up a gold spoon, but at the first touch the melon leapt off the plate and disappeared under the table.

I sat crimson with embarrassment while it was retrieved by a disdainful footman with powdered hair, and another piece placed in front of me!

SIR HUGH CASSON

Left-Overs

Meals are memorable to me not for the food and drink (I am no bon viveur), but for the company, the setting and sometimes the drama. 'Memorable' does not necessarily mean enjoyable, and although I have been lucky enough to enjoy hundreds of dinners there is only one I remember for the strength of its atmosphere.

I had been asked to dinner by somebody I had not met to discuss a drawing project. 'Come early,' he said, 'as my wife has to leave directly after coffee.' The home was handsome, the meal enjoyable, the host and hostess politely talkative. If it seemed slightly uneasy I was soon to discover why. After coffee my hostess rose, apologized for leaving, said goodbye and left the room. My host explained briefly that she had 'left' in the most serious sense – suitcases and all – and would not return.

HENRY COOPER

Boxing Clever

I was at a dinner where the great 'Dickson Wright', the well-known surgeon was speaking, and in the middle of his speech 'Wee Georgie Wood' got up from his table and walked straight in front of the top table. Dickson Wright stopped talking and watched him walk the full length of the table. In deadly silence Dickson Wright turned to the mike and said 'Yes, he'd cut very tender.' The whole room erupted in laughter.

An elaborate feast for a lady of quality, from a French fifteenth-century illuminated manuscript. By this period, the presentation of the food, like the architecture and costumes of the French nobility, was becoming increasingly sophisticated and self-consciously formal. Meals were governed by strict ceremonial, served by a hierarchy of retainers and accompanied by specially composed music. Note the musicians' gallery and the sideboard for the proliferating types of pewter and silverware.

On the Edge

It was one summer, probably June or July, with Lord Rupert Nevill, known to my wife Kath always as 'the other Rupert', at Horsted Place, Sussex.

There were about eight or ten at a round table in the dining-room for lunch on this Sunday, with Princess Margaret as Guest of Honour, seated on my left. The butler was serving sangria to all of us, but when he came around to Lord Rupert Nevill, he served him with a very nice white wine. Kath who was sitting next to him immediately declined the sangria and said 'I would rather have some white wine.' Lord Nevill insisted that it was only for him, but 'I will share my bottle with you only, darling.' The rest of us had to stay with the sangria.

Unfortunately, during lunch I upset my glass, which had just been filled, and to my horror a tide of red moved slowly towards Princess Margaret, who had a very attractive white bouffant dress. We were all rather close together and I was endeavouring to stop the encroaching sangria before the butler could come round to assist. There was no way anybody could move, but fortunately my efforts were successful and the tide of sangria stopped on the edge of the table.

As you can imagine, it became a most hilarious lunch as Lord and Lady Nevill were old friends and Princess Margaret was able to relax and spent the afternoon sunbaking.

Chinese dining practices and menus have remained intensely conservative, as this tenth-century painting, now in the Palace Museum at Taipei, shows very clearly. The simple elegance of daily life in the T'ang imperial court, illustrated here, is similar to the best practices in contemporary Chinese

JOAN COLLINS

Too Many Dinners

One can eat too many dinners. When I was making *The Bravados* in Mexico, co-starring Gregory Peck, the director of the film insisted that I do all the riding myself, without making use of a double. My horse, Pancho, was a great deal of trouble: a mixture of terror and boredom (there is always some of the latter with film-making) had driven me into the arms of the great pacifier Food!

Every night the hotel served pecan pie, my favourite dish. Every night I would persuade the jovial Mexican cook, who loved my appreciation of his food, to give me the left-over pies. I took them to my lonely, prefabricated, Holiday Inn Mexican-style hotel room with the single fifteen-watt light bulb, put on the record player and gorged. To the sentimental ballads of Sinatra, Tony Bennett and Johnny Mathis I devoured slice after slice of pie until, like some early Roman glutton, I fell into an exhausted nightmarish sleep, filled with grinning, ghoulish, red-eyed fearsome horses, ready to eat me along with their bales of hay. The next morning I'd stuff what remained of the pie with the script and finish it off as a little mid-morning snack. After ten days of this gluttony, the wardrobe woman unsuccessfully tried to zip me into the pants which, tight before, now fitted like a sausage skin.

My midnight feasts did not go unnoticed. The director decided to use a riding double as often as possible, hoping that this would relax me and keep me away from my pecan pie. They even got a double for Pancho! Eventually I gave up the pie and started playing cards at night.

A drawing by John White, from the late 1500s, of 'Coastal' Indians eating. White arrived in North Carolina in July 1587, as part of an expedition sent by Sir Walter Ralegh; a month later his granddaughter, Virginia (named, probably, after England's 'Virgin Queen' Elizabeth I), became the first English child to be born in North America. White soon set out for England for supplies, but on his return in 1591 found no trace of the colony he had left behind save the word 'Croatoan' (the name of one of North Carolina's coastal inlets) carved on a tree. The colony may have gone off with friendly Indians, such as these, possibly from the Hatteras coastal tribe.

The man in this drawing wears a single wild turkey feather in his hair – the bird was introduced to Europe from North America in the early part of the sixteenth century, and is now the staple of Christmas in England and, in America, of Thanksgiving Day, which originally celebrated the Pilgrim Fathers' first harvest in New England in 1621. It is difficult to be sure what 'meate' (in those days a generic term for food as distinct from drink) the Indians are eating, but it is probably hominy, maize kernels swollen by soaking and boiling, still used in the southern states as an alternative to potatoes and rice.

Theire sitting at meate

JILLY COOPER

Dog's Dinner

A Persian meal being prepared at an oasis in the desert, with all the equipment a modern cook might require – chopping-board, stoves, large mixing-bowls and, above all, plenty of hands to make light work. When the Arabs swept into Persia, they acquired a taste for many of the latter country's favourite dinner recipes. These included jellies, sweet flavours mixed with meats, and the use of ground nuts to thicken their dishes. Before long the Arabs had carried these new tastes into lands they conquered or colonized, including Europe. So far as English-speakers are concerned, the greatest Persian exponent of eating and drinking was the late-eleventh/early-twelfth-century poet, astronomer and mathematician Ghiyathuddin Abulfath Omar Bin-Ibrahim al-Khayyami, 'the Tent-Maker', better known as Omar Khayyam, a part of whose Rubaiyat *(a collection of* rubais, *quatrains, numbering some 500 in all) appeared in an English translation by Edward Fitzgerald in 1859. The book was almost immediately remaindered, but in 1860 Rossetti discovered it, closely followed by Swinburne, and with their support* The Rubaiyat of Omar Khayyam *slowly achieved great fame. It is widely held that Fitzgerald – whose Persian was, frankly, not up to much – traduced Khayyam's serious purpose, producing instead a work of which one of the principal themes is 'eat, drink and be merry.' Of Khayyam, Dawlatshah wrote in 1487: 'He was a tentmaker first. Then an astronomer. I believe he wrote some verses. He also was bad-tempered and exceedingly inhospitable.'*

Doris Potter was a beautiful black Labrador-type mongrel who belonged to my husband Leo's cousin Philippa. Doris Potter adored her mistress only slightly more than food.

One day Philippa's husband had a smart dinner party of foreign clients, but the wife of the most important guest couldn't come because she had 'flu. Doris Potter sat in for her to stop there being thirteen at the table, and spent the evening with her head on the guest of honour's dinner-jacketed shoulder. Everything went well until her mistress got up to get the pudding from the kitchen. Doris Potter, who had sat too close to the table in her greed, couldn't bear being separated from her mistress and crashed all the length of the table after her, sending flowers, candles, glasses, plates and everything flying.

'Tis the Voice of the Lobster

Every few weeks, the craving comes for a three-day Riviera hog and, since BA343 whisks one door-to-*porte* in less than four hours, why, we have always cried as the knife rattles in the piggy bank slot, spend twice as much on one of those English gourmet weekends which inadequately fabricate the authentic? Especially given the decor in which they do it: while I yield to no one in my admiration for Colefax and Fowler, they cannot hold a candle to Alps and Mediterranean.

There I was in Nounou, fish restaurant nonpareil, corner table overlooking Golfe Juan, orange moon overlooking me, and anticipative nostril overlooking the *soupe de poissons*. It is a joyous dish, not least because you can play with it: it evokes the days when you dug ravines in porridge mountains and sent warm syrup rivers coursing through them. You launch the toast discs in the soup, pile the *rouille* aboard, sprinkle the grated cheese thereon, and eat the ones that capsize first. (Don't look up *rouille* in Cassell's, it offers only *rust*, *mildew* or *blight*, God knows why. Probably Cassell didn't get out much, had a Marmite sandwich on his desk, who can say?)

Anyway, I was happily splashing about in my dinner when I noticed a lobster come up at ear-height. It hovered over the

The illustrator of this Italian treatise on household management of 1549 has concentrated on cooking ingredients, including plucked fowl ready to be roasted on the spits or on the grid on the elaborate brazier at the centre. In the foreground, the kitchen boy is working the bellows, while the servant at the left prepares the pastry. The equipment used here to prepare dinner is of a fairly rudimentary kind, the batterie de cuisine *being a sharp knife, a ladle, a cauldron, perhaps a trivet and sometimes a spit. It was in sixteenth-century Italy that table forks were brought into use for eating meat, although they had been used in the Middle Ages, mainly in southern Europe, for eating sweet food such as fruit in syrup. The English traveller Thomas Coryat commented on this novelty in 1608: 'This forme of feeding I understand is generally used in all places of Italy, their forkes being for the most part made of yron or steele, and some of silver, but those are used only by Gentlemen. The reason of this . . . is, because the Italian cannot by any means indure to have his dish touched with fingers, seeing all mens fingers are not alike cleane.'*

The Battle between the Lean and the Fat, the title of this panel, probably refers to a proverb of some kind. Pieter Brueghel often chose such subjects and this painter was one of his followers. The fracas depicted may have been the sequel to a memorable dinner by the gluttons. In England, the land of compromise, the proverb, current by 1639, related not to a battle but a truce: Jack Sprat could eat no fat/ His wife could eat no lean/ And so between them both, you see/ They licked the platter clean. *Although salted or smoked meats were monotonously frequent items on the menu for the better-off in northern Europe, there was much more opportunity for a varied diet in regions near rivers or the sea: note the abundance of seafood scattered across the floor.*

next table, waving and having a last look around the way they do, and having got the approbatory nod from the plump diner beneath, it was borne off to the kitchen.

The plump diner was not alone. With him were his wife, a teenage daughter, her younger sister and, youngest of all, a little boy of perhaps four. It was even as my wife and I were murmuring − the way the English invariably do − about the charm, manners, turnout and, above all, sophistication of French tinies at the nocturnal table, that the boy began first to sniff, then to weep. His mother reached towards him, but he turned sharply away, muttering between sobs; whereupon his father leaned down, ear to the trembling lip, and, having listened, pushed his chair back and marched briskly out.

Readers who can smell happy endings a mile off will know what happened next. After perhaps a minute, the lobster came back, not this time in the waiter's grasp, but in the father's. What was going through the lobster's mind at this point is not easy to guess, but if it was occupying itself with the unpredictability of biped behaviour, it was not far wrong. The father's other, unlobstered, hand now took hold of the little boy's and, Nounou's doors giving out directly on to a shingle beach, the three of them proceeded outside, crunched along the strand to, a few yards off, a little jetty and, having walked to the end of it, launched the father's erstwhile entrée into the sea.

I had half-expected that when the pair came back into the restaurant the other diners would applaud; that they didn't may be attributable either to the fact that many of them were sitting in front of plates piled with embarrassing dismemberment, or that the shock of watching a man send 200 francs swimming towards Africa had irremediably compromised their approval.

The Yellow Room

Until 1952, when my mother finished restoring the King's Room from a kitchen back to a small dining-room, the Yellow Room was the dining-room at West Wycombe.

My earliest memory of it is when my sister Sarah and I, after lunch in the nursery, were made to dress in our smartest clothes to salute the guests. We were ushered in by one of the footmen in maroon tailcoats and black and gold striped waistcoats, and after a curtsey from Sarah and a bow from me, we had to say *'Bonjour Messieurs'* and *'Bonjour Mesdames'* and then go round the table shaking hands or getting a pat on the head – quite an ordeal.

As we grew older we had our meals at a separate table for *'la jeunesse'* in a corner by the window. One of our ploys was to stare at my grandmother when the strawberries, freshly picked from the garden, were being handed round, to embarrass her from taking too many as there would be none left for us.

During the war the dining-room became a sort of restaurant for all the people staying in the house. Wartime rations were very small, and we resorted to eating coots and moorhens which were cooked in aspic and served cold. On one occasion we even decided to shoot a swan. My brother John and I thought it rather unsporting to shoot one on the water so our old keeper, Low, chased them round in a punt until they took off over the waterfall, below which John and I were stationed. Luckily we got one, but we then had to pluck it, which took most of the day and filled two large bags with feather and down. The following week I invited a party of friends from Eton and we sat down in the dining-room and ate the whole swan.

An al fresco dinner in the countryside, with a small town in the distance. One of the guests plays a flute, another a lute, while the others are enjoying the company. A servant brings the food; the beer is in the flagon marked with the engraver's initials in the foreground.

SIR ROBIN DAY

Moderation in all Things

In 1976 I was due to conduct a long TV interview with Harold Macmillan, his first intervention in contemporary politics since he had resigned as Prime Minister.

In advance of the interview, Macmillan took me to Buck's, one of his seven London clubs. Sipping Buck's Fizz, for here was where that delicious drink was invented, we considered what to eat. 'Would you like to start with some oysters?' Trying not to sound too eager, I replied, 'That would be very nice.' Macmillan then asked, 'How many would you like?' Then, happily, before I had time to reply that half a dozen would be fine, he said, 'I think six is too few, and twelve is too many. So how about nine?' At this, emboldened by the champagne, I risked a little repartee: 'Of course. How wise! *The Middle Way*?' This allusion to the title of Macmillan's famous pre-war book on economic policy made him smile.

This highly coloured sixteenth-century engraving shows a well-heeled group at dinner – note their swords, the splendid hanging lamps and the metal vessels on the buffet at the right. Judging by the way the guests are holding their food, the dogs will do well.

LEN DEIGHTON

It may be Memorable, but is it Dinner?

Déjeuner. Jeûner means to fast. So literally déjeuner means to break the fast or breakfast. Artfully the French have managed to arrange some eating before breakfast so déjeuner now means lunch. So what about *dîner*? In medieval times those who were rich enough to eat big meals ate the biggest one of the day at about 9 a.m. Since then the main meal has been served later and later. One book (*Description of England*, William Harrison, 1587, 2nd edition) says the English had only two meals per day and describes the variations in meal times. Harrison says that until then many people had eaten four times a day and admits somewhat disdainfully that there were still '. . . here and there some hungry stomach that cannot fast till dinner time'.

Now, he says, nobility, gentry and students have dinner at 11 a.m. and supper between 5 and 6 p.m. Merchants, especially those in London, a shade later; at noon and 6 p.m. Husbandmen 'dine at high-noon as they call it, and sup at seven or eight'. Out of term, he says, university scholars dine at 10 a.m. 'As for the poorest sort they generally dine and sup when they may, so that to talk of their order of repast it were but a needless matter.'

Today most people eat between 7 p.m. and 9 p.m. But is it dinner? In France, as in Britain and Ireland and other places

More interested in the formal garden than in the guests, Sebastien Vrancx (1573–1647) depicts a feast in the park of the Duke of Mantua. The guests have probably dined in the loggia on the right and are now enjoying fruit and wine – kept cool in the vessel in the foreground. Others look down on the scene from the roof terrace on the right and from a window on the left.

too, people who eat their main meal at midday call it dinner (dîner). In France's rural areas the evening meal is often called la soupe or souper (supper). If a Frenchman asks you to join him for a pot-luck meal (a most unlikely possibility, may I add, since the French are reluctant to invite people into their homes, especially for an informal meal), he would say, *'Venez manger la soupe avec nous?'* This association of soup with evening meals means that many chefs of the traditional school do not believe that soup should be included on any proper lunch menu.

LORD DENHAM

A Lost Opportunity

It was early in 1945 and I was in Brigade Squad, the first phase in the conveyor belt system for the production of Guards Officers. Caterham was full, for the moment, so my particular squad was in a camp on Sandown Park racecourse, but part of the course was a long weekend spent in learning the intricacies of the army motorbike. We were to be billeted in a large ivy-covered country house not far from the Devil's Punchbowl in Surrey, and we were decanted there late one evening from the back of an army three-ton lorry. A quick evening meal and we

A feast on the edge of a lake by Giovanni Donducci (1575–1655). Elaborately prepared food is being set out on the table, while the wine is being cooled in the foreground. On the left, two of the guests are washing their hands before dinner – this was much emphasized by Renaissance courtesy books since most eating was still done with fingers. In the Middle Ages, each diner would mop up the grease with a trencher, a roughly cut thick slice of stale bread. Napkins were introduced in the Renaissance, but were often treated with little respect; people also wiped their hands on the table-cloth.

were loaded back into the three-tonner and taken off to a pub in Hindhead. The whole thing had a holiday atmosphere about it. Our temporary home, we were told by friendly locals, was reputed to be haunted by the ghost of Oliver Cromwell.

Late the following afternoon, we were issued with our motorbikes and taken out on the road for the first time, in parties of four with an instructor. My party brought up the rear.

It was a lovely sunny day, the birds were singing and, at first, everything went swimmingly. Then, after driving through a village, we passed a gateway from which a herd of cows was on the point of emerging to cross the road. The instructor and the three pupils in front of me had passed by the time the leading cow stepped out. She and I looked at each other, both pausing politely for a moment and then simultaneously starting forward again, whereupon my front wheel collided with the cow's hind legs and both cow and motorbike subsided onto the tarmac. The motorbike promptly stalled, but the cow unfortunately did not. Gathering herself up and, at the same time, casting a look of intense reproach in my direction, she crossed in front of me, followed closely by the rest of the herd.

By the time that I managed to restart the engine of the motorbike, the last cow had passed and I was able to see the road in front of me again, stretching out far, and totally empty, ahead. Even by the time I reached the next crossroads, the rest of my little convoy was nowhere to be seen. I tried going straight ahead first, which seemed at the time to be the most likely direction, then back to the crossroads, taking the left turn for several miles this time, then back again to try the right – all with equal lack of success. By this time I was hopelessly lost and the sensible thing would have been to go back to the house where we were billeted but my difficulty was that I had no idea at all as to what it was called or where it was situated. If anybody has ever ridden a motorbike for hours around the by-roads of Surrey, enquiring of each all-too-infrequent passer-by as to the whereabouts of an anonymous ivy-covered house that was haunted by Oliver Cromwell, he will have just an idea of how incredibly silly I felt.

I was now getting hungrier and hungrier. The rest of my squad would by this time be sitting down to their evening meal – meat stew, accompanied by soggy greens and mashed potatoes, perhaps, with plum duff and custard to follow – and it began to assume in my imagination a degree of gastronomic excellence that one would nowadays only look for at the Connaught Hotel. Eventually, there seemed only one course of action left to me. I did remember the name and the approximate location of the pub to which we had been taken the night before, and where we were due again later that evening, and I made my way to it, deposited my motorbike in the car-park and went into the bar to wait miserably for the arrival of my friends.

I am still grateful for the way in which they contrived to temper their amusement with slightly uncharacteristic sympathy at my predicament and, as I remember it, there were no official recriminations afterwards. Perhaps the officer commanding the course had a sense of humour too – but I never did get that evening meal. I yearn for it yet.

The Wedding Feast *by Jan Brueghel I (1568–1625). Then, as now, important family occasions took place to the accompaniment of copious quantities of food and drink. One matriarch seems to have a covered wickerwork chair all to herself, and the bride and groom are to her left. In the foreground, boys are running to fetch even more wine, which is being decanted into stoneware flagons. It is not clear why there are quite so many halberdiers present – perhaps the groom is a soldier, or perhaps they are members of the 'watch', an early form of police, their presence demanded by the need to deter gate-crashers. Certainly some of the villagers on the wrong side of the wall seem to be keenly interested in the proceedings. The bagpiper has been exiled to the branches of a tree, an action which many English people would heartily applaud. Jan Brueghel, sometimes known as 'Velvet Brueghel', was the younger son of the great Pieter Brueghel I ('Peasan Breughel') and brother of Pieter II ('Hell Brueghel'); his father painted another – famous – wedding-feast scene, as well as* The Land of Cockaigne, *in which the sated diners are shown sprawled out.*

The Language of Food

I have been lucky enough in my life to have been to some unforgettable dinners, the reason for remembering them usually being pleasurable. But one stands out as a kind of nightmare and I shall always think of it with a mixture of misery and shame.

I was staying with my sister Nancy Mitford in Paris. We were invited to dine with a friend of hers who was Président du Conseil Constitutionnel. The party was in his official residence in the Palais Royal. It was always a pleasure to go into this glorious building with its golden rooms and paintings borrowed by our host from national collections.

On this night the guest of honour was Monsieur Pompidou, then Prime Minister of France. I found myself sitting next to him. I discovered, to my horror, that he couldn't (or wouldn't) speak a word of English. I can't speak French.

Never have four courses of delicious food taken so long to be served and eaten. There was no escape, no way round. All we could do was crumble bread and smile at each other, while my discomfiture was the cause of much merriment to our host, who sat immediately opposite us across a narrow table. He knew our limitations perfectly well and did it for a joke.

An early meeting of the Bruges Group. The painting, by Anton Claessissens (c. 1538–1613), actually records a banquet held in Bruges in 1574, attended by civil servants and the captain of St Janszestendeel. These town dignitaries have reached the fruit course and are drinking wine from elegant silver-gilt tazze, served from heavily ornamented ewers – bottles with corks were still a rarity and non-U at table – and cooled in the vessel on the left. The servants appear to have been dressed as Roman soldiers for this occasion. In the background, the women are enjoying a banquet of their own.

JASON DONOVAN

A Good Chew

This detail of A winter feast at the Bavarian State Palace, by Hendrik van Balen the Elder (1575–1632), shows a superabundance of delicacies of every kind, combined with rich furnishings, exotic birds and the most refined accessories for eating. Seated at a table groaning with food, one of the diners appears to be holding a small fork; to the right of the musicians is a buffet with fashionable silver-gilt vessels and façon de Venise glass. The procession to the table includes a black servant carrying a boar's head, while in the foreground a pet monkey is advancing on a plate of waffles.

Note the hare and other game, of which venison was especially highly prized — indeed unscrupulous vendors would often offer beef that was high, wrapped in a pasty, as venison.

I travelled to Osaka in August 1990 to do a series of promotional appearances for my Japanese record company. After casually agreeing to consume some of the local delicacies on one of Japan's highest-rating television programmes, I was presented with a platter of very unusual-looking morsels. The programme went live to air and also had a rather large studio audience. I had not visited Osaka before and I was keen to make a very good impression.

The compères of the show were two young Japanese guys who didn't speak any English at all. I was lucky enough to have a translator beside me who was trying to explain what I was about to put into my mouth.

I got through a couple of dishes without any trouble at all until I encountered something which was a little difficult to chew. I tried to chew as quickly as I could as I was aware of the camera pointing straight at me. Just at that time I caught a glimpse of the two compères who had a look of terror on their faces. I think they thought that I couldn't swallow whatever it was I had in my mouth and that I was going to be sick. Unfortunately I broke into hysterical laughter and spat the entire contents of my mouth over one of them. He was wearing one of the nicest suits I have ever seen.

As I was dying of embarrassment and the compère was flicking pieces of chewed octopus from the lapels of his very expensive suit, the audience broke into uncontrollable laughter. My record company told me later that I had made 'a very funny joke' and that the appearance was a great success. Strangely, I have not received a request to appear on the programme again!

Speak Up

Robert Morley's father-in-law was Captain Buckmaster, who founded the famous Buck's Club in London. Robert is therefore an important figure within those walls. Some years – in fact many years – ago I wrote a play in which it was my ambition to have Robert and Wilfrid Hyde White as my two leading actors. They both differed from this view because – as I think – neither of them could decide which of the two leading parts was the best one. Therefore, when I asked Robert to play Sir Lionel (a Foreign Office dignitary on a visit to Rome), he developed the theory that the part of Sir John (the British Minister to the Vatican) was the better part. And, Wilfrid, needless to say, thought the reverse!

They were both wrong, of course, but their respective viewpoints prevented either of them acting in it.

However, Robert asked me to Buck's for a meal with himself and Wilfrid, in order to break to me their final decision not to do the play. It began as a sad meal, since I forced them to tell me their decision at the start, but it became hilarious later on.

This happened when, the thorny and disappointing point having been disposed of, Wilfrid began talking very loudly indeed about some other subject than the theatre – racing, perhaps.

As I recall, at adjoining tables there were plenty of Guards Officers behaving impeccably and talking in a normal civilized manner.

Then, after a particularly violent oration by Wilfrid lasting a couple of minutes, Robert remarked 'Lower your voice Wilfrid, this is a gentlemen's club!' 'Is it, me boy?' said Wilfrid; then he added: 'Nothing written up to say so anywhere.'

Oh dear, oh dear.

In this scene from the life of the Prodigal Son, by Louis de Caullery (c. 1580–1621), eating seems to have given way to philandering. One of the women is offering her companion a drink from a long-stemmed stangenglass, *a type fashionable in Germany and the Low Countries in the seventeenth century.*

The parable of the Prodigal Son (Luke 15: 11–32) was a popular subject with painters. The younger of two boys, the Prodigal Son asked his father for his share of the inheritance and took himself off to a far country, where he wasted his money on riotous living. Flat broke, and in the midst of a famine, he got a job as a swineherd and, starving, eyed the pigs' miserable food with envy. Finally, he set off for home, where his father was so pleased to see him that he ordered a fatted calf to be killed for a feast in his honour. Then, as – generally – now, goat was the staple meat of the area, beef being rich man's food.

LEN EVANS

From the Sublime to the Sublimer

Name-dropping, to start with, there was a seven a.m. phone call from the then Prime Minister of Australia, Malcolm Fraser.

'Russian eggs,' he bellowed, for he is a very big man.

'I beg your pardon?'

'You soft boil the eggs, then cut off the top and stuff them with caviar. . . .'

'Sir,' I said. 'I do know what Russian eggs are, but what about them?'

'Well,' he replied. 'First course for dinner. Go well with the Montrachet.'

He was referring to the inappropriately named *Single Bottle Club*, so called because all members each year supply their best bottle. This began in 1977 as a tribute to Michael Broadbent MW, the famed public palate and head of Christie's Wine Department who was paying his first visit to Australia. Malcolm Fraser was there and the oldest bottle was a 1727 Rüdesheimer

This fragment of a larger Flemish painting (the rest is lost) depicts preparations for a grand dinner in about 1620. Peacock, boar's head, and probably a swan or two would have been commonplace. On the buffet is an opulent display of glassware, silver and silver-gilt. The parakeets are not for the pot.

Apostelswein. One of my staff, a great chap who has gone on to better things, was decanting it when there was a fearful clatter. The silence that followed was the end of the world, broken by 'Oh, I *am* sorry. Shall I open the 1728?'

So we had Russian Eggs at the Lodge, the official residence of the PM in Canberra, at the '82 dinner, and that night the outstanding wine was 1865 Lafite, given to me by the late Jean Troisgros, that marvellous cook. It opened in magnificent order, and a week later I read that another bottle of it had sold at an auction for US $10,000. So I sent a copy of the report to all members and asked them what they intended to donate the next year.

The 1980 dinner featured a 1646 Tokay, the oldest wine I've ever tasted. I had special glasses blown to commemorate the occasion and when we drank the wine, tears came to my eyes as I reflected on the passing of the human parade while this wine lay waiting in its bottle.

1990 was my sixtieth birthday and we drank '29 Krug, six D.R.C. le Montrachets, seventeen D.R.C. Romanée Conti vintages back to 1952, their first wine after the re-planting of the vineyard, six d'Yquems back to '22, and three ancient Australian reds, including an 1855 Hunter. My slight headache the next morning was the most expensive I've ever had.

I've not mentioned food much. Please accept from me that the food at these dinners is quite wonderful, equal to any in the world. That sounds like a typically Aussie boast, but we do have marvellous ingredients and our young cooks work all over the place – France, Italy, Hong Kong, Tokyo. The result is an entirely flexible feast with all sorts of influences support-

If there is a common theme, besides food and drink, which links the depiction of meals, it is music, as this painting of An Elegant Company at Music Before a Banquet *by Hieronymus Janssens (1624–93) shows. The seventeenth-century equivalent of an hostess's 'fashion accessory', the black servant, is also plainly in evidence. Whether music truly aids digestion, as some believe, or is 'the food of love', as Shakespeare averred, is a moot point.*

ing the originality of each particular chef in charge.

On one occasion Gerard and Françoise Potel arrived in the Hunter Valley for a simple lunch. He is part-owner of Château Pousse d'Or in Burgundy and a noted maker of fine Volnay and Pommard wines. Lunch was great fun, as we tasted and drank many Australian wines. Later that afternoon we visited the Rothbury Estate, of which I'm Chairman, and examined some Chardonnay and Pinot Noir wines in which he was especially interested. A couple of bottles of bubbly and back to the house to say au revoir.

Somebody, however, arrived with a huge fresh fish. Why not cook it later and carry on the day? By this time fine old bottles were appearing and guessing-games began. Then someone started singing and we all joined in. One chap even sang all the arias from an opera, doing all four major parts and most of the duets, though the quartets did seem to lose something in his translation. Finally lunch finished at midnight, a twelve-hour affair of great happiness.

In the morning I counted 37 empty bottles. That was between ten people and, I can swear to you, on my oldest bottle of Hine (Grande Champagne 1949), that no one was drunk that evening. Happy, intoxicated even, yet full of life and all joy.

Probably the most memorable meal I ever had was when I was cold and wet and hungry. Four of us were lake fishing for trout in the Australian Alps and the weather had turned nasty. The fish were down and nothing enticed them. Then someone put a horrible green-red thing on his leader, a cross between a large wet fly, a huge nymph and a small frog. Still fishing with a floating line, he dispiritedly cast onto the lake. When I was young, I had a car called God because it moved in mysterious ways. Well, this could well apply to trout for, after a totally fruitless morning, this horrible fly had only just dipped under the surface of the water when it was hit by an express train. Fifteen minutes later a magnificent four-pounder was landed, a rainbow trout, in the thickness and plumpness of top condition.

Quickly we gutted and cleaned the fish and rolled it in wet newspaper, four sheets of it, each piece being individually wetted and wrapped around the fish so there were umpteen layers. While this was being done, a small brush fire was somehow lit, and the fish went straight on it. No coals are necessary, for the newspaper acts as a steaming jacket and, though the outside layers dry and eventually burn, the inside ones stay moist.

Another twenty minutes or so, and the paper was peeled off carefully. It took the skin with it to reveal the moist, succulent, steaming flesh. This was taken from the bone and placed on slices of Dr Vogel's bread, of the nutty wholegrain kind, spread with unsalted butter. Fresh-ground black pepper on top (we fish fully armed) and the fish was eaten straight away. The wine was an old Hunter Semillon from 1960. They age magnificently, acquiring a deep green-gold colour, a fragrant nose and huge depth of flavour.

This wine, the fresh bread and butter, the great trout, eaten within forty minutes of being landed, on that day of biting wind and ice-cold rain, sitting miles from anybody by a lake on top of Australia, remains one of the most memorable meals of my life.

The Great Kitchens at Hampton Court Palace, restored to illustrate the feast of St John the Baptist on Midsummer Day 1542, when Henry VIII provided lavish entertainments for his court. Among the delicacies on offer were wild boar, peacock pie, red deer pasties and baked carp, as well as a marzipan confectionery in the shape of St Paul's Cathedral.

In one year, the Tudor court ate its way through more than 1240 oxen, 8200 sheep, 2330 deer, 760 calves, 1870 pigs and 53 wild boar, washing this down with 300 barrels of beer, together with quantities of wine and mead (a fortified wine sweetened with honey). Understandably perhaps, the Tudor kitchens at Hampton Court are the largest and most complete kitchens in Europe from this period, a sprawling complex of more than 50 rooms.

MICHAEL FRAYN

Strain Cook Thoroughly Before Serving

When I was a bachelor I used to dine variously on fried eggs, fried bacon, fried eggs and fried bacon, or fried bacon and fried eggs. There were also occasional days when I had forgotten to buy either eggs or bacon.

My somewhat limited range in the culinary field has earned me but a menial position in the kitchen now that I am married. I am allowed to peel the potatoes and empty the trashcan, provided I stand to attention when spoken to, but not to prod the soufflés, or baste the beans, or whatever real cooks do.

There are, however, certain recipes which reduce my wife to such a state of nervous disintegration that she is forced to lean on me abjectly. I mean the sort written by authors who haven't yet heard the good news about the invention of weights and measures. And if a recipe-writer still hasn't got round to the concept of ounces and pints (or for that matter hins and cubic cubits – we're prepared to make every effort to compromise), you can bet your bottom tea-leaf that he hasn't managed to grasp the principle of written communication either, or of predicting what tools and materials he is going to need until he has actually picked them up.

I hear despairing cries from the kitchen, and find my wife set on making a recipe which starts off: 'Pour a fair amount of milk into a medium-sized bowl, and throw in a generous handful of soya beans. Add a modicum of grated cheese and the quantity of chopped chives which lie on a sovereign piece.'

I help my wife choose a particularly medium-sized-looking bowl, and supply the generosity for measuring out the soya beans. 'Take a few eggs,' the recipe goes on, 'and carefully separate the whites from the yolks. Now whisk them into the mixture.' The whites or the yolks? We compromise with a half of each.

'Fry the mixture for a few minutes over a hottish flame, until it is the colour of a walnut sideboard, and there is black edging round the shredded onion.' The shredded onion? 'This should have been added before the soya beans in order to prevent the milk curdling. Now quickly transfer the mixture to a cast-zinc stew-pan.'

'Run out to the corner,' shouts my wife, 'and buy a cast-zinc stew-pan.' I run all the way there and back. 'You'll have to go out again,' she cries on my return. 'After I've transferred the mixture to the cast-zinc stew-pan I've got to add a very large eggcupful of icing-sugar.' Without a word of protest I run all the way back to the corner and get the icing-sugar. 'No, no, no!' shouts my wife as I stumble breathlessly back into the kitchen with it, 'I've got the icing-sugar – I wanted you to buy the very large eggcup.'

When I stagger painfully back into the room again with the eggcup, I find my wife sieving tiny pieces of raw meat out of the mixture. 'The recipe,' she sobs, 'says: "Pour the mixture over a jam-jarful of minced beef."'

'Then why are you taking the beef out again?'

'The next sentence says: "The beef should have been roasted for an hour first."'

We force-roast the beef, and brace ourselves for what lies

The artist Jan David de Heem (1606–84) found the food so luscious in Antwerp that, being a specialist in 'still-life' viands, he felt compelled to move there in 1636. It was, he said, 'in finer condition and ripeness to draw from life' than food found anywhere else in Europe.

ahead. 'Place an asbestos mat beneath the dish,' says the recipe, 'and beat it with a wooden spoon. Continue beating until, at the bottom, the top of it is covered underneath with a grey sauce of sodden soya bean. The bottom of it should then rise out of it, coming through the top of it (the pan) until the rest of it (the bottom of it) can be separated from it, and placed in a pie-dish beaten to the consistency of thin gruel. Bake briskly. When a fine blue aromatic smoke begins to rise, the mixture is hopelessly overcooked.'

It is quite late at night when the fine blue aromatic smoke at last curls out of the oven, and we are both very tired and weak with hunger. My wife turns over the page and reads the

last sentence of the recipe: 'Before serving, store in a cool place for at least a fortnight to allow fermentation to finish.'

Well, well. But the canned luncheon meat, I must admit, is opened to a turn.

SIR NICHOLAS FAIRBAIRN OF FORDELL

Good Memories, and Less Good

The best meal that I have ever given at Fordell Castle was one Sunday when we celebrated the seventieth birthday of our beloved daily lady – Mary Walker – who is otherwise known as the blonde tornado. We played a 'This Is Your Life' trick and all her family were there before her, though she thought she was just calling in to pick up her presents. We had Coronation Chicken and other delicacies and all greatly enjoyed a happy afternoon of fun and stories and laughter. I have never enjoyed myself so much in the presence of royalty, judges, the grand or the grim, whom I have entertained in this Castle.

Monkeys Feasting by Ferdinand van Kessel (1648–96). This is a satire on the sin of gluttony and may well have been intended as decoration for a dining-room, in a vein of ironical humour. The painting above the fireplace draws a parallel with the human condition. Note the kitchen implements, including a spit and pan to catch the fat, and the device for hanging game.

The King Drinks *by David Teniers the Younger (1610–1690) is another parody of upper-class life, the peasantry aping their 'betters' and, generally, looking a great deal happier in their carousing. Although Court Painter and Keeper of Pictures to the Archduke Leopold Wilhelm, Regent of the Netherlands, Teniers specialized in scenes of peasant life and achieved immense popularity, with over 2000 paintings ascribed to him. These 'genre' paintings were probably popular with rich aristocratic and bourgeois patrons because they satirized gluttony without bringing the lesson too close to home.*

One or two other dinners, which I admit I enjoyed greatly, involved ordering people to leave my table because they were offensive. These were always people I did not know and who had either been invited by others, or were in the house for the first time. I do not permit people at my dining-table to be offensive and so some of the most memorable dinners I have ever had have been those when I have required some of the guests to abandon the house.

On a happier note, I recall the occasion of our entertaining our Bishop to see if he would give permission to marry us in our own chapel – both of us being divorced. I discovered that my wife had given the Bishop a pillowcase instead of a napkin. Fortunately the pillowcase was empty, which is perhaps why he gave us permission.

We have at Fordell a great tradition of entertainment. My wife Sam is a magnificent cook, the dining-room is very beautiful and the guests are chosen to be great fun. Eating, as any new-born baby realizes, is the most important urge in life and the dining-room at Fordell has always given the greatest of pleasure in the service of mankind. After dinner we circulate and change places so that the congregation and conversation is shared amongst all those who come to dine.

SIR RANULPH FIENNES

What an Act to Follow

As European representative of the late Dr Armand Hammer, Chairman of Occidental Petroleum Corporation, I was once invited to speak on behalf of the guests at the Annual Dinner of the Institute of Petroleum. Never having attended before I had no idea of what was in store. I assumed it would be a rather chummy affair where a few general comments would suffice for a speech.

A week prior to the event, I phoned the Institute to find out who would be the Guest of Honour, so I could prepare my address accordingly. I was told they were as yet unsure who it would be. When the evening was nigh, I was still uninformed, so I assumed it would be the Chairman of one of the main oil companies.

The first shock was the size of the occasion. Fifteen hundred worthy oilmen and their guests packed the Great Room of Grosvenor House, resplendent in their black ties and, where relevant, their decorations. The top table was raised on a high platform and floodlit. My mouth was already dry as the shamal wind.

'She has arrived,' the Director of the Institute announced with excitement. I was lined up beside an entrance as Mrs Thatcher arrived in a royal blue evening dress. She looked radiant. She was fresh from a party conference in Brighton and a narrow escape from an IRA bomb at her hotel. Security dictated that no one knew her schedule in advance.

Anticipation ran high during the dinner and the announcement of her speech was met by a thunderous roar. She was highly amusing and, looking over her shoulder, I saw that her most entertaining lines were when she departed from the prepared notes.

The PM talked for a good ten minutes, but much of the time was taken up by ecstatic applause from her audience. She ended by apologizing that she must leave at once, which she did to a standing ovation that continued a good few minutes after she had gone from the room.

It was then that I had to speak. If I could have vanished from the face of the earth at that moment I would willingly have done so.

LORD FORTE OF RIPLEY

Guest of Honour

If I had been told when I first arrived in Britain, as a bewildered child holding my mother's hand, knowing no one and unable to speak a word of English, that years later I would celebrate my eightieth birthday in the grandest of style with a dinner party for over 1000 people, I would have thought it was a fairy story.

In fact, the night of 22 November 1988 was a fairy story.

There beneath the shimmering crystal chandeliers of the Great Room at Grosvenor House they assembled to give me a welcome so sincere that I could feel its warmth as I accompanied the principal guests to their places at the top tables.

In seventeenth-century England meals went on for a long time for those rich enough to afford such a lifestyle. These diners are described as card players in the reign of James I. As a result of the voyages of exploration of the previous century, they may well have been tasting the delights of new foods such as turkey, aubergines, tomatoes, followed by apricots, figs and mulberries. Sweet potatoes had also arrived on the English menu. At such fashionable gatherings, roasts and grills were ousting the medieval pottages. Pies, like the one on the table, might contain live frogs or birds. Here, however, the main preoccupation is the wine, and there is evidence that the wines of Spain (such as 'sack', white wine from the Canary Islands) were as popular as those of Bordeaux, then as now called 'claret'.

Everywhere I turned there were familiar faces I knew and loved. My devoted wife, our son and five daughters, my brother and sister and their families, close friends and colleagues of a lifetime – and a distinguished guest list drawn from all walks of life.

The guest of honour was the Princess Royal and my health was proposed by the Prime Minister of the day, Margaret Thatcher, a lady for whom I had and still have the highest regard. I was very touched when she said: 'I don't think there is anyone in the country who has as many friends as Charles Forte.'

At the dinner I was honoured by the launching of a new foundation in my name, aimed at helping people in the hotel and catering industry acquire new skills by establishing awards and bursaries, a cause dear to my heart. In every way, it was for me a most personal occasion.

The meal itself was magnificent. A kitchen brigade of fifty prepared a special menu with the maître chefs of four of my favourite hotels supervising individual courses; from the Ritz in Madrid there was goose-liver terrine with artichokes and truffles, from the George V in Paris turbot with white chicory, from Grosvenor House in London guinea fowl in a juniper sauce and from the Hotel des Bergues in Geneva a sweet of caramel ice, chocolate and hazelnut cream.

While it was being served there was music from the orchestra of the Scots Guards and, as I cut an enormous cake, another old friend, Dame Vera Lynn, sang 'Happy Birthday'.

There was a lump in my throat that evening, but it did not stop me eating and enjoying what was the most memorable dinner of my life.

CHRISTOPHER FRY

Anniversaries

12 February 1964: I was staying with Philippe and Pauline de Rothschild at Château Mouton. John Huston was staying there too. I was writing the script of a film which he was directing. It was a spring-like day, warm and still. In the morning I had worked with Philippe on my translations of some poems he had written, and afterwards I walked through the vineyards with John Huston as far as Château Lafite, talking about the film. There was another walk in the afternoon when Philippe and Pauline joined us. 'The sun set red,' my diary says, 'and the air was cold.'

Dinner that night was in Petit Mouton – meals were taken in one or other of the two houses as Pauline decided. I don't know why I didn't keep the menu; I had done so on two other days, February the 9th and 10th. On the 10th the diary says: 'after the excellent 1921 claret came the really extraordinary Mouton Rothschild 1870, six years from achieving its century, which surpassed any wine I had ever drunk before.' But February the 12th also has its place in my memory. John Huston was born in 1906. I was born in 1907. Our birth year wines were brought from the cellars. The 1906 almost rivalled the 1870. It accompanied the meal as Ariel partnered Prospero – 'dearly, my delicate Ariel'. But my year was judged to be a poor bottle and was sent away from the table, to be replaced (as we all are) by a younger wine, 1953, Coronation year.

Was it on one of these three February days, or on a return

A feast given by Louis XIII at Fontainebleau (1633), engraved by Abraham Bosse (1602–76). Here there are about three large plates in front of each guest, from which each would help himself and pass portions on to his neighbours. Note also the sauce-boats and salt-cellars. The host sits in lonely state at a separate table; he is the only diner to be waited upon, although his guests may be attended by their own servants. It was in the middle of the seventeenth century that the French, whose dining habits up till then had been immoderate, changed their style of eating and began to replace their groaning tables with subtler offerings. By the next century, their cookery books had turned eating into a matter of philosophy rather than of necessity.

visit to Mouton later in the year, that the Swedish ambassador, when talking about the English theatre, mentioned several times someone called Clarence Tarragon? It took me a little while to realize that he was a man I called Terence Rattigan.

The nearest I came to my own birth year had already been drunk on February the 9th, a Mouton Rothschild 1909. To celebrate my existence I give the menu for that evening's dinner:

Consommé aux moules
Cailles flambées
Purée de petit pois
Fonds d'artichauts farcis
Foie gras a la gelée
Salade
Fromages
Les trois glaces

Mercurey 1959
Mouton Rothschild 1945
Mouton Rothschild 1929
Mouton Rothschild 1909
Yquem 1949

Those vintage years cover a fair swathe of my life:

1959: I had been to America and exchanged it for Italy.
1945: I began writing a play in peacetime.
1929: I was midway in a three-year stint as a schoolmaster.
1909: I first went into short trousers instead of petticoats.
1949: *The Lady's not for Burning* opened in London.

SANDY GALL

Lunch in the Desert

'Come and have lunch on Friday,' my Saudi friend said on the telephone. 'In the desert. I'll get someone to pick you up.'

In due course, I was fetched by a charming young British diplomat and driven to the house of an English brigadier who advised the Saudi National Guard. This was the rendezvous point from where we set off in convoy, driving through the outer reaches of Riyadh, the capital, a huge sprawling city reminiscent of America, designed for the Cadillac and not the camel.

I rode with an old friend, feeling rather grand perched up high in the front of his Range Rover, and soon we were batting along one of the many superb six-lane highways which link the principal cities of the desert kingdom. Apart from the military convoys speeding north and east of the desert – for this was just before the start of the Gulf War – the road was almost empty. About twenty miles out of town we turned right into the desert and followed a broad, bulldozed track across the sand. I was surprised to see a wire fence running down both sides of the road, but my friend explained.

'It may just look like empty desert to you and me, but it all belongs to someone. So do the camels.' There they were, floating almost ethereally above the desert floor, chewing disdainfully at a few small grey bushes that somehow managed to grow in this inhospitable environment.

We drove perhaps ten miles and then turned off again on to a rougher softer track which wound through the dunes. In the distance there were signs of a camp – a tent or two and a compound containing some spirited-looking Arab horses and a small herd of camels. Within a few minutes, we had arrived and were being greeted by our host, Prince Abdullah, a charming man in his forties who had done an engineering degree at Nottingham University and then, bravely, worked on the shop floor of a local factory. The mind boggles at the sort of English humour he had to put up with. Remarkably, he seems to have survived unscathed, and perhaps even more surprisingly, still seems to like the British.

He greeted us warmly, closely shadowed by a servant in bedouin dress who poured each new arrival a small cupful of Arabic coffee, bitter and rather weak. One of the other guests, a Saudi, explained, 'You know why they only give half a cupful?'

'No, why?'

'It comes from the days when we were very poor. When we couldn't afford much coffee. That's why it's weak and they still only pour half a cup.'

Given the vast wealth of the Saudis today, I thought this was a rather touching little story.

I swigged it down and handed the cup back. The man promptly filled it up again. I remembered then. If you don't want a refill, you either wiggle the cup from side to side or hold your fingers over the top of the cup. When you do that the coffee-pourer takes your cup and slides it on top of the other empty cups in his hand, with the hollow chink which is one of the gratifying little sounds of everyday life in the Middle East.

More and more guests arrived, until we were a large animated group, standing about on thick carpets spread on the sand in the pleasant winter sunshine. Like any party anywhere, except, of course, there was no drink.

At one point several of the Prince's British and Saudi male friends had an animated discussion. One of the Saudi guests wanted to know from everyone in turn the answer to the question: 'Is there going to be a war?' He quizzed us one by one, starting with the Brigadier who paused briefly, and then said with complete conviction. 'Yes, I believe there will be a war.'

My friend with whom I had driven out was next. 'Yes,' he said. 'I agree. I think there will be a war, too.'

Next he turned to me. 'What do you think, Sandy?' Putting on my rather boring journalist's hat, I prevaricated. 'Pass,' I said. 'I'm just an observer.'

All the others said they were convinced that there would be a war, but it was noticeable that the Saudis, without exception, insisted 'not only will there be a war, but there has to be a war! We have to get rid of this bloody man!' – meaning Saddam Hussein.

Lunch was served. We trooped into another spacious tent where, on a huge mound of rice, was draped a splendid rib

Interior of an inn by Wolfgang Heimbach (1600–78). Inns were not expected to be places of gastronomic delight, particularly in the war-ravaged central Europe of the mid-seventeenth century. They served wine and simple food: meat was often presented in small portions so that it could be eaten with the fingers. Although Italian gentlemen had begun, in the sixteenth century, to hold their meat with a table fork while they cut it, this refinement was slow to spread elsewhere and the fork was said to be an affectation. Note the apparatus on the right for cooking meat at different heights above the fire.

and saddle of camel, golden brown in colour. The Prince himself carved and so sharp was the knife that he nicked his finger and had to be hastily bandaged up by a competent English lady. This was only a temporary setback. We queued up plate in hand to receive generous portions of the pale, tender meat, looking remarkably like veal. It tasted like it too, a little flakier perhaps, but quite delicious.

It was baby camel, of course, cooked in the traditional bedouin manner and the best meat I had in two months in Saudi Arabia. My only regret was that there was no Pouilly Fumé to wash it down.

JAMES GALWAY

Round & Round

Recently I was on tour with my wife Jeanne and three of my children, Jenny, Lotti and Paddy. I played a concert in Innsbruck and afterwards we went to our hotel to have supper in the beautiful old restaurant. They had a musician playing on that famous Austrian instrument, whose name I can never

remember.* I asked the children what they would like to drink and Jenny rather coquettishly asked for champagne. I ordered the best bottle in the house and we were having a splendid time together when Jenny announced to the house in Swiss German – 'Jiminy, the restaurant is turning round and round.'
*Zither!

BOB GELDOF

A Burnt Offering

The band teased Paula something rotten. 'Are you cooking Bob his dinner?' asked Fingers artlessly one day, as she was in the kitchen making some instant coffee.

'No . . . why?'

'Oh nothing . . . I just wondered.'

'Wondered what?'

'I thought you must be cooking his dinner. His other girl-friends usually did.'

'Ah no. We're, er, going out tonight. I'm cooking his dinner tomorrow.'

She had never cooked a meal for anyone before in her life. She had never even been shopping for food, except for the necessities. Usually she ate in cafés. Wishing to impress me, she took the train into London and then a taxi to Harrods and bought steaks, tomatoes, mushrooms, potatoes and a ready-made dessert. It cost her £27. She couldn't work out how people could afford to eat at those rates. Then she burned it to a cinder. I smiled grimly as I cut into the succulent carbon and told her it was delicious. It would become a regular spectacle in our house on Saturday evening. The band would gather in a cheery circle to watch their singer consume the latest burnt offering.

Large houses and religious establishments obtained an all-year-round supply of meat from the birds who lived and bred in their dovehouse. A foreign commentator wrote of England: 'No kingdom in the world hath so many dovehouses.' This one is still alive and cooing in Oxfordshire.

Another famous Oxfordshire dovecote stands beside the ruins of the manor of Minster Lovell, in the Windrush valley. Francis, the 1st Viscount Lovell, was an ardent supporter of Richard III, who resisted the Tudor regime; it is said that a great deal of money, possibly part of Richard III's treasury, disappeared with him at some time between the battles of Bosworth and Stoke. In 1708, a secret sealed room was discovered in Lovell's manor; it was found to contain the skeleton of a man, presumably starved to death. It is thought that Lovell had hidden there and had died from starvation, but legend has it that the remains were found still shackled to the wall, with a plate of food placed just out of reach – a truly tantalizing death.

So there is such a thing as a Free Dinner

Ladies and gentlemen feasting in an elegant interior *by Melchior Brassauw (1709–57). The artist has captured the mood of the idle moments before the serious business of eating begins. With pewter plates lying empty before them, the company waits for the meal to be brought in. One woman is playing with her fork, while another is being encouraged to try the wine; the dog evidently expects to be thrown scraps once the dalliance is over. The servant is carrying a ham, which had been a delicacy since Roman times, when the best varieties were imported from Gaul (France).*

I first met Elizabeth Taylor when I was directing the Burton *Hamlet*, just after they were married in America. She was extremely kind to me, but the whole atmosphere was so charged with hysteria when they came to Boston just after the wedding that they were literally torn to pieces, and the plane had to be moved to another part of the airfield when the crowd pulled their hair and clothes.

One night in Toronto, during the weeks of try-out before taking *Hamlet* to New York, I wanted to give them supper because they had been so nice to me, and I engaged a table at some little downtown bistro run by a Czech. We had about eight bottles of champagne and then a very good supper. But when we came out, at two in the morning, there were more than a hundred people in the snow waiting to see the Burtons. The next day when I went back to pay the bill they would not give me one. I said, 'Well at least let me tip the waiters,' and they said, 'Oh no, our boss did that last night. It's been such a good advertisement for the restaurant.' So it was the cheapest entertaining I ever did in my life.

SIR NICHOLAS GOODISON

Bon Voyage

I was in Strasbourg giving a talk to a large audience of members of the European Parliament, officials from the European Commission, industrialists and others. My subject was deregulation and the need to press on with measures to ensure competition in goods and services across the whole Community. I spoke particularly of the need for a single currency. The Chairman of the meeting, Lord Plumb, the ex-President of the European Parliament, remarked to the audience that it was my first visit to Strasbourg. I hope that it was his fatigue following a flight from South Africa the night before which led him to add 'and I hope it will be his last.'. . .

LORD GOODMAN OF THE CITY OF WESTMINSTER

Sobering Up

A dinner I remember was one arranged by me to raise funds for the newly re-established ICA. The guests of honour – now both dead – were Jennie Lee and George Brown. The evening became 'memorable', in the sense of being easily remembered,

Although one lady is standing up, this painting by Marcellus Laroon the Younger (1679–1774) is described as representing 'ladies and gentlemen feasting at table'. It seems more likely that the four gentlemen, still wearing their swords, may have been eating and drinking prior to a little dalliance with the opposite sex.

From early times in England, mussels, oysters and shellfish were part of the ordinary diet as, of course, they were in other parts of the world. For example, it is known that the inhabitants of Catalina Island, off California, were heavily reliant on a diet of mussels in the fourth millennium BC and that shellfish also nourished the poorer classes in China from early days. By comparison, in the mid-nineteenth century, apprentices in Glasgow rioted throughout the city, complaining that they should not have to eat salmon on more than three days a week.

because George Brown, alas, was very drunk at the outset of the proceedings, and steadily got more drunk – until he collapsed across the table in front of a very indignant Jennie, who certainly did not approve of drunkenness. George Brown to his credit left the dinner-table on his own feet, and when I finally took farewell of him he could have denied ever having touched a drop of the stuff.

LORD GRADE OF ELSTREE

A Salute

One of the most memorable dinners of my life was on Tuesday 18 April 1975, when I was given a tribute dinner by the United States National Academy of Television Arts and Sciences at the New York Hilton Hotel. They called it 'A Salute to Sir Lew Grade' and had invited all the people who had been important to me during the development of my career.

The Earl Mountbatten of Burma was the Guest of Honour and had flown in specially for the night to make the tribute to me.

All my family and closest associates and friends were with me, and after the dinner there was a Cabaret with top performers whose careers I had been very much involved with. Among them were Julie Andrews, Tom Jones, Dave Allen, Peter Sellers and John Lennon, who had specially rehearsed an act for the occasion. After Julie Andrews had sung, and prior to my receiving the Award, she had primed the orchestra to strike up my old signature tune – The Charleston – to spur me to dance. Naturally I couldn't resist the challenge.

It was one of the most emotional evenings of my life and I shall never forget it.

LUCINDA GREEN

West Meets East

The Eastern Bloc and life without freedom have always intrigued me. One of my most memorable evenings was in Bucharest, Romania, in October 1990.

Thirteen of us had just finished delivering goods to orphanages from the 16-ton trucks we had driven over from the UK.

The last evening we were being shown the revolution hotspots by our interpreter, a very well-educated lady by the name of Victoria. Her husband had been thrown out of Ceaucescu's cabinet because her brother had defected to Austria. She took us back to her home to meet him. In comparison to others in Romania, they lived comfortably – but it did not compare to the West.

It was dinner-time. Of course they could not offer all of us a meal. So for an hour we sat around the fire drinking nasty red wine and eating equally unpalatable stale plain biscuits. We listened transfixed as Victoria's husband related his involvement in the happenings of the revolution (he was arrested twice). The history of those days that had so intrigued me over Christmas 1989 was told. In an extraordinary manner, every frame of action was frozen in his mind. It was indeed an unforgettable evening, witnessing so closely a corner of the history that has revolutionized the balance of the western world.

This oyster feast (detail), by Jean François de Troy (1679–1752), is being enjoyed by grand company in France. A toast is being drunk; note also the wine cooler with plates stacked inside it. A German visitor to London describes how oysters were in great demand also in Billingsgate. At an inn there 'the tables were laid with white cloths, and there were delightful wicker chairs to sit in. A fisher-woman with a basket of oysters, a youngster with lemons and a small basket containing bread, plates and knives followed immediately after us . . . I liked them very much.'

Exporting Is Fun

Hogarth's sardonic painting of an Election entertainment in 1755 (detail) is memorable for the candidate's attention to a large quantity of oysters – necessitating in turn the attentions of a surgeon to him. Oysters were not the expensive delicacy they are today. Perhaps introduced to Britain by the Romans, they had long been common even among the poor – in 1728 they were selling at only two pence a gallon. The upper classes liked them too – Pepys mentions that he began a fine dinner with them, and he would buy barrels as presents for his friends, as did Dickens's Pip in the nineteenth century.

I was engaged in an extremely tricky negotiation in Japan where we had sold some know-how which did not perform as expected. We had warned the Japanese customers that they were getting in at a very early stage, before the technology was fully proven. But relying on a combination of their belief in our technical virtuosity and their own self-confidence they ignored our advice. I was duly summoned to attend at their factory on the Inland Sea and arrived not looking forward very much to our subsequent talks.

Things did not start too well since I was put up in a Japanese inn (normally a source of great delight) and summoned to dinner. When we sat down, the very first thing that was proffered to myself and my hosts looked like, and indeed was, a dead sparrow. Not for my Japanese friends any of the niceties of plucking or de-gutting the beast or, as far as I could see, even cooking it. It lay stretched out in an advanced state of rigor mortis, with its beak firmly pointing upwards at one end and its feet protruding at the other, I looked with some dismay at this, which I assumed to be a great Japanese delicacy, and wondered how to tackle it. My Japanese hosts motioned to me to start and I really did not have the faintest idea since, apart from chopsticks, there was nothing available to tackle the beast with.

After a rather impatient pause, my host picked up the bird by its legs, popped the entire thing, feathers and all, into his mouth and chewed with evident contentment. After what seemed an age, there was a plop as he spat out the beak and,

after another suitable period, he dropped two well-cleaned legs and feet beside it, muttering something which I took to be the Japanese for 'delicious'. One of the problems in being an international salesman is that you have to suffer for your company, but I have to say my technique at eating fully feathered sparrows lived up to the highest traditions of export capability.

MAX HASTINGS

Smoked Salmon for Breakfast & Cellos for Dinner

Iceland is one of those places the world has not yet found out about, where barely a quarter of a million inhabitants tenant the coastal fringes of a great wasteland that is otherwise given over to birds. In summer, the midnight sun provides continuous daylight. Icelanders possess all the Nordic charms, and seem to save the Nordic melancholy for the dark months. And what food. Smoked salmon for breakfast no doubt palls if you stick around long enough. But for anyone passing through, fish and smoked lamb and marvellous cakes are memorable fare for the evening.

One dinner I recall was hosted by a prominent local businessman who entertained us to a barbecue on the beach under the midnight sun. This was on one of the many islands off the coast and our host also owned the tiny local church. He had arranged for a cellist from the Iceland symphony orchestra to make the four-hour trip from Reykjavick to play Bach for us, accompanied by her husband on the organ. We sat twenty-strong in the painted pews, the sun still blazing in the evening light outside, wholly enchanted.

DENIS HEALEY MP

Serving One's Country

The only exception to my rule that difficult decisions were best taken with food was the first G-5 dinner over which Mike Blumenthal presided in Washington. Because President Carter was still puritanically opposed to anything which might be regarded as luxurious living, we dined that night in a dark and cavernous room at the top of the State Department building with no central heating; we shivered with cold as the waiters brought in one atrocious course after another. My Treasury adviser said it was the first time he had ever seen me push my plate away uneaten. Mike was new to the job; he did not yet know his colleagues, or how to guide such a meeting to a decision. So one after another we simply recited our positions; the last speaker was another newcomer, the Japanese Finance Minister, who rejoiced in the name of Hideo Bo. He read out a prepared statement in Japanese for a whole hour. After another hour for the English translation, we departed without a further word to bed, well after midnight, chilled to the marrow, and with acute indigestion.

La Politesse

I was having dinner on a glorious summer evening in the open air at a delicious restaurant along the harbour front at Antibes in the South of France. Finding that our large table had run out of butter, I beckoned to a tall managerial-type lady in a bright yellow dress standing in the open doorway to the restaurant proper. She looked at me, smiled back charmingly and remained motionless. Convinced that she ran the restaurant I beckoned to her much more vigorously to come over to our table. Looking somewhat surprised, she did so and leant over my shoulder. In my best, most polite French I then demanded of her:

'Du beurre, s'il vous plaît.'

'Oh no,' she replied, 'I'm from Colwyn Bay.'

MAJOR DICK HERN

A Racing Certainty

One day in autumn 1986 Sir John (Jakie) Astor arranged with me to come and see his horses and to stay and have a bit of a meal afterwards. When I told Sheilah, she said 'Oh, let's see if Gordon would come over as well.'

Sir Gordon Richards had then reached a time of life when he did not go out much, but when he heard that Jakie was coming, he agreed to join us.

Gordon arrived just as we got back to the house and he was looking really well and full of fun. When we got into the house we had a bottle of champagne and Gordon was soon telling us amusing stories of days gone by. One story was typical of Gordon's gamesmanship.

Fish of a different kind are being swallowed in this drawing in pen and wash by Rowlandson, which was published as an etching with a verse attack on Sir Joseph Banks, President of the Royal Society, in 1788. He was accused of excessively favouring his own interest, natural history. Banks appears on the right, gnawing a serpent, and the poet urges him:

Sir Joseph, pray don't eat an Alligator
Go swallow something of a softer nature.
Feast on the arts and sciences, and learn
Sublimity from trifle to discern.

The Westminster Calf's Head Club

Coffee-houses were the ancestors of London clubs as popular dining resorts for the middle and upper-class man. The oldest surviving London club, White's, was founded as a chocolate-house in 1693. Lloyd's of London also originated as a gathering of merchants for business or gossip in the coffee-house kept by Edward Lloyd in Tower Street, London, the earliest mention of which is in the London Gazette for 18 February 1688.

The Calf's Head Club, not always decorous in its behaviour, was a republican club established in Westminster in the mid-seventeenth century. Its principal meetings were held on 30 January of each year (the anniversary of Charles I's execution), when dishes were served each symbolic of some hated aspect of the king's life and reign: a cod's head to represent Charles the man; a pike representing tyranny; a boar's head, representing the king's preying upon his subjects; and calves' heads to represent Charles as king, and his adherents. An axe (Charles was beheaded) held pride of place on the table, and a copy of the Eikon Basilike (a book purporting to contain the late king's thoughts and meditations, published on the day of his death) was burned at the end of each banquet; the club's toast was 'To those worthy patriots who killed the tyrant.' The club met in secret after the Restoration of Charles II in 1660, and seems to have survived until 1734. At that date, however, the diners were mobbed and the ensuing riot put a final stop to their meetings.

'One Derby day,' he said, 'I met Captain Allison, the starter, in the weighing room when I arrived. He said to me "Hello Gordon, my wife is coming today and she doesn't often go racing, do you fancy anything that I can tell her to have a pound on?" "Well," I said, "I think I shall win the first." The race was only five furlongs. When we lined up I came into the tapes as hard as I could go and got a flier, as I knew of course he had to let me go!'

I asked Gordon 'Did you win?'

'No, I got beat a short head!' he replied.

I can picture him now when we saw him off, as he drove out of the gate for the last time in his usual style with the gravel flying! A week later Gordon Richards, twenty-six times Champion Jockey, was no more. He died from a heart attack whilst shaving in the morning.

JAMES HERRIOT

The Vet's Story

My most memorable dinner had its beginnings in a veterinary visit to a farm in the Yorkshire Dales fifty years ago. It was to a 'blown' cow. This occurs when the animal eats too much fermentible food and the stomach becomes so filled with gas that it literally blows up like a balloon: the cow can die quickly if the condition is not relieved.

The farmer, Mr Weatherall, was understandably worried, because his cow was certainly in extremis – so blown that it was staggering about and I could have played a tune on its drum-like flank. However, I quickly made an incision and passed a little metal tube into the stomach which allowed the gas to escape in a great whoosh, giving the animal immediate relief.

Mr Weatherall was delighted and grateful when he saw his cow returning quickly to normal, so much so that he invited me to his silver wedding celebrations on the following Saturday night.

I happily accepted and on the appointed evening I presented myself at the village institute which was packed with nearly a hundred Dales farmers and their wives. It was to be a buffet-style dinner and along one side of the room a long trestle table was laden with a variety of foodstuffs which were strange and wonderful to a young Glaswegian like myself.

It was all home produce and baking. In those days every farmer kept pigs for family consumption and every kitchen was hung with hams and sides of bacon. I always had to duck my head while crossing the floor. Tonight, the table sagged under the farmers' wives' creations of piggy delicacies. Mountains of pork pies, spare ribs, sausages, quivering bowls of brawn. Whole

The first public coffee-house was opened in London in the mid-seventeenth century and by the end of that century there were over 2000 such establishments in the city. These were strictly male preserves. Women had coffee served at home, as in this picture of Mme de Pompadour, and before long coffee after dinner became the fashionable practice. Tea, however, was the opium of the masses and was also favoured by some of their superiors, such as Samuel Johnson.

hams, red and succulent, with the ladies standing by them with their sharp carving knives. Great chunks of bacon, too fat for my taste but delicately powdered with golden crumbs, and the jars of piccalilli to help it down. Close by lay roasts of beef, jellied tongues, ham and egg pies, mounds of potatoes and vegetables.

The dessert side had not been neglected, and trifles, topped with several inches of thick cream, rubbed shoulders with bowls of fruit and jugs of more cream. There were jam tarts, curd tarts, iced cakes, sponge cakes – more than I can describe. A massive Wensleydale cheese, about a foot high, dominated the far end of the table.

In one corner a barrel of beer was in constant service as the men topped up their pint glasses. I have a picture of it all in my mind to this day: the red-faced farmers at the long centre table effortlessly demolishing the delectable fare and refilling their plates again and again, the babel of conversation, the laughter and the feeling of friendship. The food was all delicious – one of my first experiences of Yorkshire cooking and a revelation to a city-bred young man. But what made it even more memorable was a remark from my host towards the end of the evening.

Mr Weatherall came up behind me and glanced along the table. The ladies were nearly all finished and sitting with their cups of tea, but most of the men, though slow-moving now and looking replete, were still plodding on – spooning up the trifles, cutting off slabs of cheese and refilling their beer glasses. He whispered confidentially in my ear.

'I just hope you've got your knife with ye, Mr Herriot,' he said. 'Because I think some of these fellers are goin' to get blawn.'

French food was beginning to catch on in London – Pepys enjoyed going 'to a French house to dinner . . . A mess of potage first, then a couple of pigeons à la esterve, and then a piece of boeuf-à-la-mode, all exceeding well seasoned, and to our great liking.' A century later, Rowlandson may have been caricaturing those who embraced the French way in this etching entitled The Disappointed Epicures *(1787), who had to endure that terrible experience of seeing their dinner on the floor. The term epicure was used to connote gluttony from about 1775 and this etching was published in 1787.*

DON HEWITSON

Vintage Stuff

Dateline: Sydney February 15 1979. There I was attempting the impossible: selling French wine to the Aussies and buying the local wines to pour down the throats of my London customers. In those days the Brit's knowledge of Australian wines was limited to the Monty Python 'Château Chunder' sketch, which was presumably researched from glasses of 'Empire Fortifieds' at a certain chain of northern wine lodges. And, whilst the Downunder slurpers were not averse to 'a bit of frog stuff', they were not particularly keen on taking instruction from someone from 'bloody London . . . especially a bloody Kiwi at that!'

Anyway, at this moment life certainly had a number of compensations. It was around 40°C on my hotel balcony and the airmail edition of *The Times* had a photograph of huge snow-drifts and stranded cars in the middle of Highgate, my home in London, where the temperature was precisely 46° short of my present abode. In the spirit of George Washington, and most politicians since, I had to acknowledge the fact that the official object of my overseas fact-finding trip was of no particular importance. The day before had been spent, along with many of the other days of supposedly conducting my 'business', attending to more important details. I had witnessed the final rites of the Australian Cricket Team as John Emburey and Geoff Miller mesmerized the opposition's leaden-footed batsmen to wrap up the Ashes series 5–1 in our favour. Our biggest-ever series victory. Ah, those were the days . . . I wonder if they will ever return? And, yes, there were more delights to come. This very night I was being taken out to dinner by an old girl-friend.

Sydney, already one of the most vibrant of cities, had recently caught the international food and wine bug. The place was awash with local wines. 'Hunter Valley Riesling' was not bad at all (no matter that there was no Germanic Riesling flavour and the wine was made from the French Semillon grape . . . it certainly washed the barbecued prawns down in fine style.) Unfortunately the dozens of different varieties of 'Chablis' were nowhere near so appealing, as this was 'BC' (Before Chardonnay) when the stuff was usually made from the Italian workhorse Trebbiano. There were many more serious delights with wonderful flavours, and correct names, but the wine-drinking public of the moment treated them with suspicion. That was great. It left more for Derek Nimmo and me!

DAVID HICKS

Getting the Wind Up

The most memorable dinner I can remember was one with the Hon. Mrs Edward Ward and my wife under canvas, but on Persian carpets, on a mountain top at Lalibella in Ethiopia, as the guests of HIM The Emperor Haile Selassie.

Extraordinarily good wines were brought up by our mule train and very good food was served on fine French china. As the liqueurs were being served, I became nervous of the tremendous wind outside and, wanting a little fresh air, went out – where I saw the pegs for the tent had been replaced by Imperial servants straining at the ropes!

FRANKIE HOWERD

From Bottom to Top

In April 1958 I was appearing as Bottom in Shakespeare's *A Midsummer Night's Dream* at the Old Vic and I must say I was rather surprised to receive an invitation to attend the *Evening Standard* Drama Awards at the Savoy Hotel.

I was thrilled but very nervous about attending such a glittering occasion. The stars in their finery, sumptuous meal, plenty of drink – then the awards ceremony including about fourteen speeches, all of which I thoroughly enjoyed after I had relaxed. Suddenly, at the end of the speeches I was handed a note – 'Would you mind saying a few words?' This was from the then boss of Beaverbrook Newspapers, Sir Max Aitken. I looked over at him with eyes which must have exuded fear and desperation as I frantically shook my head. He grinned and immediately announced me.

I have never had a clue to this day what I said or rather tried to say. I must admit I got a lot of laughs, although what I was trying to say was meant to be serious.

Every year for the next twelve years I was invited back to these wonderfully glamorous evenings, on every occasion making a speech, and sometimes presenting the Awards – in other words, doing a free cabaret act. But I didn't mind – the sumptuous repast was well worth it!

Though my appetite never declined, my career did and, by the time we reached early 1962, I had to face what was to me a heart-breaking fact – I'd had it! After the pantomime which I was doing at Southsea I had not got a date in the book – as we used to say – and no prospect of one, and so I decided to face up to reality. I thought it would be a good idea to make a start by declining that year's invitation to the *Evening Standard* Drama Awards, mixing with the great stars in the West End,

Another strange dinner is being eaten by John Bull, traditionally, if erroneously, associated with beef eating. The fact is that the majority of the population had little opportunity to eat much meat – except pork – and certainly not beef. This cartoon by James Gillray (1798) satirizes the amount of money being spent, at Nelson's behest, on the Navy instead of on food for the population at large. The Navy's reliance on salt pork for rations was itself also a cause of trouble.

These Persians are drinking coffee or, in Arabic, gahwah, which originally meant wine. Since wine was forbidden by the Koran, coffee became their wine. Although the bean had been known to be edible for centuries before, the invention of infusion after roasting was only made in the thirteenth century. From Aden in the fifteenth century, it reached Constantinople where the first coffee-house was established in 1554; one hundred years later the first such establishment in Britain was set up in Oxford by a Jew from Turkey. One of London's most successful coffee-houses was set up by an English merchant who put his Greek servant, Pasqua Rosee, in charge. A Swiss visitor to London explained: 'About Twelve, the Beau Monde assembles in several Coffee Houses. . . . At Two we generally go to Dinner . . .'

and thereby say 'goodbye to all that'. It was to be for me a symbolic gesture.

So I wrote a polite letter saying how sorry I was I could not attend it, explaining that as Southsea was full of snow and ice, I could not make the dinner in time.

I trudged out in the snow to the post-box with the letter in my pocket and trudged back with it still in there. I thought, 'Why not doll myself up and make a grand farewell appearance?'

That year I was asked to present an Award to four young and brilliant gentlemen for a review entitled *Beyond the Fringe*, Peter Cook, Dudley Moore, Jonathan Miller and Alan Bennett. I did some of my old gags. These four had never seen me perform before and actually laughed.

Now at this time they were connected with a famous satirical night club called 'The Establishment', and Peter Cook asked me to do a stint there. At this Club, my old friend Ned Sherrin saw me and asked me to appear in his television show 'That Was The Week That Was'.

So I owed much to the *Evening Standard* and all the others concerned for my rescue – so to speak – from oblivion, and I have always been grateful.

Incidentally, at the next year's *Standard* Awards, I myself received one! My my!

Since then I have often berated myself for forgetting to post letters – *but it isn't always a bad thing.*

BARRY HUMPHREYS

A Gorey Story

About fifteen years ago, I was staying at the Windsor Hotel in Melbourne when the 'phone rang. The man on the other end of the line apologized for disturbing me and wondered if, by a lucky chance, I might be free to join him for dinner that evening at a nearby restaurant. He explained that he was a publisher's representative and that one of his firm's authors, the American essayist Gore Vidal, was on a brief visit to Melbourne and the dinner was to be in his honour. The publisher mentioned that the only other persons present would be his wife and a well-known feminist journalist, an acolyte of the Australian thinker Dr Germaine Greer. Since I had nothing else on that evening, I eagerly accepted in order to meet across the table the notorious and lapidary author of *Myra Breckinridge*.

The restaurant our host had selected was one of the more old fashioned in an old-fashioned city. It had been one of the first Italian establishments before the war, long before Melbourne boasted some of the best Italian restaurants outside Italy. It served one kind of spaghetti: bolognese, and although minestrone was unavailable, there was 'minestrone soup' on the menu. Indeed, there were traces of 'minestrone soup' on the flock wallpaper as well. The atmosphere was very quiet. Elderly waiters shuffled around bearing dishes which had lost all traces of their Italian accent. Indeed, except for the watery spaghetti, they were mostly hearty Australian meals

Rowlandson was not unaware of how the other half lived, as shown in his sobering painting of the Asylum Dining Hall. Here, most of the inmates were probably hungry most of the time, as were many of Britain's rural poor, even those who lived 'on the parish'. Unlike the rich, they had, at most, two meals a day.

Italianized with a liberal garnish of tomato sauce and grated cheese. For some obsure reason, perhaps the proximity of a Roman Catholic cathedral, this restaurant attracted men of the Cloth and the occasional nun, and as I entered that night and scanned the tables for a sight of the famous author, a priest looked up from his tinned ravioli and a Mother Superior and her chaste female companions peered curiously at me over their t-bone steaks à la napolitana.

A small, rather dessicated man in a navy blue double-breasted suit sprung towards me nervously. It was the publisher's representative and he was clearly relieved to see me. I was led to a banquette and introduced to his little wife, the scowling feminist and finally to Mr Vidal himself. It was immediately apparent that the author had been the recipient of much generous hospitality during the day and he lay slumped in his chair, occasionally gulping from a large glass of mahogany-coloured fluid. However, our host was clearly determined that the visitor enjoy a truly cosmopolitan meal with two key members of the Australian intelligensia.

It seemed that my host and his wife had been coping with the illustrious writer all day, showing him the sights of Melbourne: the lovely originals in the National Gallery of Victoria, the Botanical Gardens, the Floral Clock and Phar Lapp, the most prodigious race horse in the history of the Australian turf, whose awesome effigy may still be viewed in the city museum thanks to the cunning of a local taxidermist. The task of entertaining the author cannot have been easy, particularly since it soon

In contrast, Rowlandson shows Dr Syntax dining in a stately home, with the footman carrying the flowing bowl, and with the inevitable dog in front of the fire. Dr Syntax was a versified grotesque clergyman who set off on tour round England in search of the 'picturesque', but it must be said that this scene sums up the English ideal of the dining-room for many years to come – perhaps even to the present day. By this period, the dining-room had evolved as a room separate and distinct from the communal hall, which had been the venue for most social activities including eating.

became apparent at dinner that the publisher's representative and his wife were totally unfamiliar with Mr Vidal's *oeuvre*. A waiter wearing a shiny dinner jacket over his maroon cardigan appeared, proffering a ragout-flecked menu and Gore, briefly roused from a jetlagged swoon, apostrophized him in very loud Italian. Unfortunately, none of the waiters in this famous Italian restaurant spoke that language though one of them was Greek. However, the guest of honour was reluctant through the evening to accept this fact and continued to address the bewildered staff in an incomprehensible tongue enquiring about their wives and families, details of their private lives and, more regrettably, their sexual vocations.

All would have been well if the distinguished and cosmopolitan man of letters had totally avoided the English language throughout the evening, but alas, seized by mischievous impulse to goad the lady journalist at our table, he proceeded to discuss, at the top of his voice and in vernacular English, certain ingenious practices then in vogue in some of New York's more liberated Turkish baths. I looked anxiously across the table at the publisher's pale little wife and observed that she had decided rather wisely to pretend that none of this was happening. She and her husband proceeded to order very large drinks and as the meal proceeded they both slid very slowly and with tremendous dignity under the table. The Melbourne feminist had begun to cry, but Gore was beginning to enjoy himself. As his roast lamb à la napolitana congealed on his plate, he began accosting some of the other diners and it was not long before

Rowlandson's The Hunt Supper *(c. 1790) illustrates the strongly male attendance at private dinner parties. While there were occasions when women dined alongside their menfolk, the rule in tribal cultures as well as in the so-called sophisticated societies more often favoured male exclusivity at dinner. Hence dining clubs, masonic dinners, rugby dinners, MCC dinners and all the other manifestations of male superiority which required that ladies either absent themselves altogether, or withdraw while the men take port and indulge in questionable anecdotes.*

Rowlandson's most formal picture is an aquatint celebrating the Patriotic Dinner held at the City of London Tavern, 14 December 1813, to celebrate 'the Glorious Event of the Emancipation of Holland from the Tyrant of France' (i.e. Napoleon).

the manager himself was politely urging us to resume our literary discussions in another restaurant. The feminist had left anyway, noisily, our host and his wife were on another plane, barely reachable even by embarrassment, but the author was incensed. As we reached the door and had our hats and coats thrown at us by an exasperated staff, he turned, and addressing the entire restaurant, shouted: 'Don't f**k around with old Gore,' turned on his heels and was gone.

I have read his subsequent *causeries*, but have discovered no reference to this visit to my home town. Perhaps he didn't remember it or perhaps he deemed it undeserving of the merest footnote, but it was certainly a footnote in the literary history of Melbourne and at least five waiters, four nuns and yours truly will never forget it.

ELSPETH HUXLEY

The Chef from the Bush

When we lived in Kenya, a key member of the household was of course the cook. I well remember how big a gap we children felt when we were told that Juma the cook had decided to return to Nairobi. He had come to us largely as a favour, for he was a townsman really; nor could Tilly and Robin my mother and father afford his wages, so they were relieved when he went. For a while the kitchen *toto* he had trained carried on very well,

Frederick II of Prussia, called 'the Great', dining with the French philosopher, dramatist, historian, and man of letters, François Voltaire; also among the guests are the French belles-lettriste, Jean Baptiste de Boyer, Marquis d'Argens, and the Italian philosopher and writer on art, Francesco, Count Algarotti. From as early as 1739 Frederick had sought to bring Voltaire to his glittering court, but when the latter eventually came, in 1751, it was not a success: the volatile and arrogant genius and the authoritarian, if highly cultured, king soon parted company, Voltaire leaving to live in Switzerland in 1753, where he died 25 years later.

This engraving by Adolph von Menzel (1815–1905) is possibly from his illustrations for Franz Kugler's History of Frederick the Great. *It is likely to be somewhat romanticized – Frederick had fallen out with Argens some ten years earlier (although he erected a monument to Algarotti in Pisa after the Italian's death), and both Carlyle and Macaulay recorded the friction between Frederick and Voltaire.*

but then he had to go away to be circumcised, and there was a hiatus filled by various birds of passage, who scarcely knew how to boil an egg.

One day, when Tilly was riding through an uncleared part of the shamba, a large red Masai in pigtails, who Tilly said was stark naked – in actual fact he probably wore the little short cloak of the warriors, which fell short of the waist – a red Masai stepped out of the bushes and raised his travelling spear. Her pony stopped dead and snorted, and she stared at him in surprise. This was some way from Masai country and she had never before seen a warrior so far from his native plains. He seemed to be alone, not with a party of cattle-raiders, and gave the normal greeting, 'Jambo!' in clear warrior tones.

She returned the greeting. 'This is my bwana's shamba. What do you want?'

'I want to be your cook,' the warrior replied.

Even Tilly was surprised at this. 'Do you know how to cook?' she inquired.

'For two years I have looked after seven hundred goats.'

At the time, she reported, this had struck her as an adequate reply. 'It didn't seem much use to ask his form on cheese soufflés, or whether his puff-pastry was really light. His repertoire will no doubt consist mainly of well-curdled milk and blood, served high, varied perhaps by a little ghee and raw steak, which I daresay is very healthy. At any rate he seemed quite resolved to come, and ran home behind the pony, his pigtails flying in the breeze.'

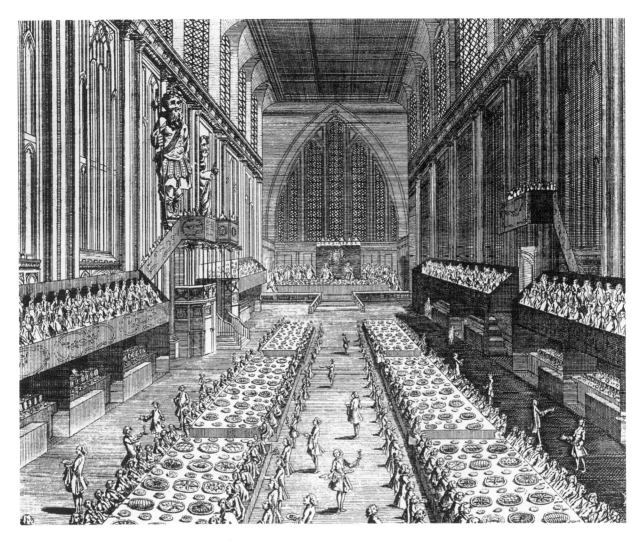

Hard to beat for sheer quantity is the banquet at the Guildhall, London, given by the City to George III and Queen Charlotte on 9 November 1761. The artist seems to have employed a degree of licence in delineating the size of the plates, and there appears to have been a paucity of cutlery.

He was not a good cook, although he had, it appeared, received a little training and was willing, cheerful and anxious to learn. With the passing of time I think I can say that his dinners became memorable even if, as my mother had forecast, they were healthy rather than gastronomic.

RALPH HAMMOND INNES

The Name of the Game

At the Lord Mayor's Summer Banquet, Dorothy and I were in line waiting to be greeted and move on to a drink. The Summer Banquet is always directed towards the arts and we had already sighted several guests we knew. Our turn came and I was suddenly faced with the Lord Mayor – clean-shaven and balding, a large, impressive figure in his robes.

'Hullo, Ralph. How are you?' I stared, my hand held out for the ritual handshake.

'*Flamingo*. Remember?'

The gilded splendour of the Mansion House, the City's dignitaries, the flunkeys, everything vanished, and in its place were the limpid waters of the Persian Gulf, smooth as silk, and a cocky young man on the bridge of a frigate commanded by my wife's cousin. He had had a beard then and was in the uniform of a lieutenant, with his naval hat worn at the rakish Beattie angle. 'Good God!' I murmured. 'Robin!'

I'm not good at names, my excuse being I invent them. But even so.... And now, meeting him periodically, I always feel slightly embarrassed, still finding it difficult to match the man of the moment with the youngster I had known in the Gulf. Cocky and bearded, he had navigated *Flamingo* through the hazed red-rock maze of Hell's Gate in the Hormuz Strait, and down the Arabian Sea to Mazira Island, where I dreamed of a book that would eventually be called *The Doomed Oasis*.

NANCY JARRATT

Les Evénements Remarquables

I was invited to become a Chevalier of a French Order of Gastronomy. The *intronisation* ceremony was to take place in splendid cellars in Champagne. 'I'm going to France to be enthroned,' I gleefully mistranslated for the benefit of impressionable friends. Then the registration form arrived: name, address, company and rank were straightforward enough and even easier was the large space for details of honours already conferred since it had, alas, to be left completely blank.

We were a very large gathering in Epernay. *Grande tenue de soirée*, the invitation said, which was interestingly interpreted by several other female guests as tee-shirt and trousers. The investiture began to a reverberating trumpet fanfare and those ahead of me stood modestly upon the platform whilst their long list of credentials was read out – Officier, Chevalier, Consul, even Ambassadeur.... Finally it was my turn. The Master of Ceremonies intoned from an immense scroll that I had served my distinguished employers well for 25 years; a long pause and then, since he clearly found this somewhat inadequate, he was inspired to improvise '*Elle est une businesswoman remarquable.*'

The Commandeur approached to invest me – probably with some trepidation, since I was not only *remarquable* but twice his height. In traditional brocade sombrero and matching dressing gown (the Order having been established at least five years previously), he looked for all the world like a medieval mushroom. I bowed low to receive a handsome medal on a taffeta sash and at that solemn moment realized that one of my foolishly high heels had become immovably embedded in the platform. How to retire gracefully? Should I appeal to the Master of Ceremonies to set aside his scroll and dig up the platform? Or nonchalantly rejoin the audience barefoot, leaving both my size nines behind? England surely expected something better of its sole representative, and so I spread my skirts and swept the Commandeur a full court curtsey, in the depths of which I managed to haul the heel out of its prison.

We repaired to another cellar for the celebration banquet. Pyramids of prawns poised upon elegant metal frames ... *hors d'oeuvres* so wonderfully *variés* we could have feasted on them

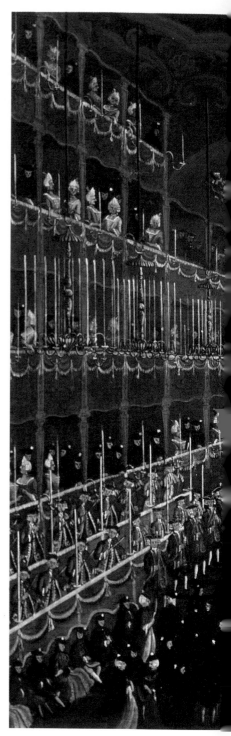

A supper given for the Dukes of the North in the Téatro San Benedetto, Venice – a painting by Gabriele Bella dating from the second half of the eighteenth century. It would appear that only the ducal party is being fed, the rest of those present being servants and spectators; the fire risk from the naked

candles, as well as the heat, must have been stupendous. The full-bottomed wig, which the upper classes had adopted by this date, is very much in evidence, although the last patrician opponent of the perruque in Venice, Antonio Corner, died in 1758 aged 84, still wearing a full head of his own hair.

alone. Coveys of smiling chefs waited to cook trout, lobster, salmon, beef, lamb to command; no narrow choice of local cheeses – the finest of all France were there – and a glut of glorious *desserts* which made gluttony seem the most understandable and excusable of sins.

'Félicitations, Madame!' cried the friendly neighbours at my table, who were sheep farmers from the Ardennes. 'Félicitations to you also,' I rejoined, noting their multiplicity of medals. '*Ah, non,*' they said, 'we are only officers but you, Madame, you are Chevalier, and your *révérence* to the Commandeur was most charming.'

HUGH JOHNSON

A Night in Gori

We had not the slightest intention of stopping in Gori. We had
been filming in a downpour all the short November afternoon
and longed to get back to our rooms and dry clothes in Tbilisi.
But it was already eight in the evening when our bus sloshed
through the scarcely lit streets of Stalin's birthplace. The driver,
a barrel with limbs, said it was too far to go on. Our minders
from Georgian state television said we couldn't stop without
authorization. But when we saw the monumental façade of the
hotel built to entertain prestigious Stalinist pilgrims, we didn't
hesitate. The five in the film crew and five Georgian friends
shouted stop, and the barrel stepped on the brake.

First impressions were encouraging. The pillared foyer seemed
brightly lit, with incongruous but rather jolly Italianate fres-
coes. With customary curtness we were told there were no
rooms, which was plainly a lie. But the concierge lacked the
spirit to prevent us trooping upstairs. While the party organized itself noisily in bedrooms that had not been occupied for
the time it takes to accumulate half an inch of dust, I took on
the rôle of quartermaster and headed for the kitchen. Experience told me that food after eight o'clock was going to be a
struggle.

The Georgian word for 'nyet' is 'ara'. It is the first word you
learn and the one you hear most often. It was what the burly
blonde waitress said to me in the many-pillared dining-room,
and the filthily dressed chef repeated it when I found the kitchen.

*Pleasant surroundings make a
dinner memorable and this
unidentified Italian artist
of the late seventeenth century
is clearly more interested in
the courtyard of his baroque
palace and its embellishments
than he is in the food. The
menu of a banquet given by a
contemporary Pope consisted of
four courses: 1. Antipasto –
olives and prosciutto; salted
pork tongues; cold, spit-roasted
songbirds; Neapolitan spice
cakes. 2. Hot roasted meats,
including game and birds such
as skylarks (still on the menu
in some Italian resorts), veal,
goat and sweetbreads. 3. Boiled
sausages, meats and stews.
4. Delicacies from the
sideboard – pear tarts wrapped
in marzipan, fresh almonds
and Parmesan and Riviera
cheese.*

A Japanese print of a Chinese dinner-party. From the teapot and cooking-pan being kept warm at bottom right, to the small bowls and chopsticks on the table, there is almost nothing in this picture that would be alien to the modern Western visitor to a Chinese restaurant. Tea reached Britain from China at the end of the sixteenth century, but by the eighteenth century relations between the two countries were so poor that the British authorities decided to introduce tea-planting to India, where it flourished; at the same time, merchants of the British East India Company were importing great quantities of opium from India into China.

Large-scale emigration of Chinese indentured labourers – 'coolies' – to Europe and America began in the 1840s, and it is from then that the West's taste for Chinese cookery developed. In Britain many of the first Chinese eating-houses (as well as opium dens) were situated in dock areas, since coolies were employed in large numbers as dockhands – one of the oldest such restaurants in London still occupies a site near the old West India Docks.

Two dozen Georgians were well advanced in their dinner at tables well furnished with meat, potatoes, salads and bottles. Vodka bottles, Champanski bottles, bottles of red wine. . . .

I began to glow inwardly, and pointed hopefully. 'Ara.' We were benighted travellers, my hands said. 'Ara.' Twelve of us, soaked and starving. 'Ara.' There wasn't much sign of food in the kitchen, it is true, since the chef was packed up and ready to leave. All I could see was a pot of cold cooked spaghetti, a huge pot, as grey and unappealing as the spare wheel we had spent half the morning fixing on the bus. I marched up to it in desperation and must have pointed to its coils with some peculiar conviction. Perhaps the chef had miscalculated and shouldn't have cooked it at all. For whatever reason his 'ara' faded, he scowled, and he switched on a hot plate.

His spaghetti recipe called for no elaboration. First you cook it into a congealed lump. Then you burn it. By the time the twelve of us were at table it was burning well, and smelling horrible. Could we have some vodka, champanski, red wine like our friends across the room? 'Ara.' Happily we had stocked the bus with a case of sharp garnet-coloured red from Imeretia while we were filming. The barrel, willing for once, took his bus keys and went off to fetch it. Now everything was ready for the feast.

The wine was fine, sharp and warming. The spaghetti, doled out on smeared greyish plates, was cold, slimy, putty-hard and singed black in parts. Salt had not entered into its cooking. There was no sauce. But the taste of burning had permeated the whole lump. The barrel managed some, but the rest of us just looked at the meat and greens on the Georgians' table and swallowed our wine.

Georgians are famous for their hospitality. We were only surprised by how long it took. A florid man in a grey suit turned towards us, stood, and launched into an enthusiastic speech – a toast, clearly. His grin at the end encouraged us to raise our glasses and drink what was left. He turned back to his friends, laughing, and they poured more champanski. We turned to our interpreter. 'You just drank Stalin's health,' she said.

LORD KING OF WARTNABY

Politics & Sport

A dinner which I remember vividly, because of a conversation which I found fascinating, is one which took place some years ago. The principal guest was the late Lord Rosebery, who must have been over ninety at the time.

I knew that Lord Rosebery had been a keen foxhunter and asked whether he had ever hunted with the Belvoir, of which I was then Master.

'Yes,' said Lord Rosebery, 'I did hunt once with the Belvoir and was sent home when the hounds checked twenty minutes from Melton Spinney.'

'You must have behaved very badly for that to have happened,' I remarked.

'No,' replied Lord Rosebery, 'I was not sent home by the Master, but by the Master's wife.'

The Master was Lord Daresbury who was the grandfather of the present Lord Daresbury. 'Oh,' I observed, 'you at that time were Lord Primrose, of course, and a Liberal.'

'Yes,' said Lord Rosebery, 'and that was the reason I was sent home.'

I said that I presumed that the incident must have occurred in 1906, the year of the Liberal landslide, and Lord Rosebery confirmed that this had indeed been the case.

This engraving by James Gillray satirizes the celebration of the Act of Union (1800), which brought together the Kingdoms of Great Britain and Ireland, and shows the predictable conclusion of a party where much more has been on offer to drink than to eat – Ireland's contribution to the new United Kingdom. On the left, John Bull (looking suspiciously like Charles James Fox) is slumped in his chair in a drunken stupor; the liveliest revellers appear all to be Irish, with shamrocks pinned to their hats.

CLEO LAINE

Singing for One's Supper

The year 1986. The place New York City. The company Princess Margaret, Carolina Herrera, Oscar de la Renta and others. Princess Margaret was in town for an official engagement for the Royal Ballet. After her duties were finished we got in touch, and I arranged for her to visit the show I was in on Broadway, *The Mystery of Edwin Drood*.

I was invited to supper at the home of her hostess after the show. Princess Margaret and I always seem to end up singing together when we meet informally and few can beat our renditions of songs both old and new. However, on this occasion we had competition. Oscar and Carolina knew all the songs in Spanish and sang them as lustily as we did in English. I think the battle was won when we came up with a song that didn't have a Spanish lyric, but I certainly remember it as one of the best sing-songs I've been involved in. Good singing too.

JAMES LEES-MILNE

An Experience of Supreme Happiness

In my books of youthful memoirs I recalled how, when my mother sent me a £1 note to spend on 'something good' for me, I decided instead to spend it on a visit to Covent Garden, where a place to stand in the gallery cost half-a-crown. It was *Don Giovanni*. Standing near me in the gallery was a young man, exactly my own age, who had just left his public school. We immediately became friends.

An experience of supreme happiness is difficult to communicate, and its outward manifestations must be banal to a third person. In the first interval we walked round the market; in the second we had a drink at the bar. When the performance was over we walked away together as a matter of course, and had supper at the Café Royal. We sat upstairs over Hamburger sausages and lager, which exhausted the remainder of my mother's pound as well as his contribution. What do rather earnest boys of eighteen talk about? I retain no accurate record of our conversation, but I know he explained how Mozart, of whom I had known next to nothing before this evening, was the purest artist who ever lived. When I complained of not understanding certain passages of the music, he said 'But didn't you enjoy them?' He was the first person to teach me that the purpose of art, and knowledge, was to give pleasure. Until that moment I was totally unaware of this basic truth. On the contrary, I had thought of art as a deadly serious matter like algebra, but for some reason best known to myself more uplifting; and a desirable thing to be approached and taken with respect and awe like the sacrament. To equate it with enjoyment was daring and revolutionary. I felt that a weight had been lifted from my intelligence.

Later we discussed in the manner of adolescents the relation of art to life, the meaning of existence and the pursuit of ideals. Having disposed of these cosmic problems we discussed

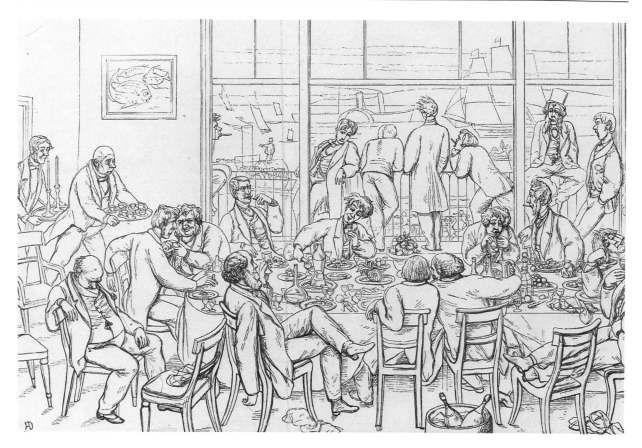

ourselves without one shred of reservation. It was like peeling two artichokes. Off came the hard, outer, protective leaves in a hurry; then the soft, inner tendrils with caution. The stark centres were exposed, succulent and ready to be devoured. It is a horribly trite thing to say, but we truly laid bare our souls. When it was time to leave I knew him and liked him better than any human being in the world.

Since he had to go north of Regent's Park to his parents' house and my direction lay westward, we parted on the steps of the Café Royal. 'When shall we meet again, Theo?' I asked, for we were on Christian name terms already. He was to accompany his parents into the country the following morning. So he replied: 'The very day I get back. I will telephone. In which case we had better take each other's surname and address.' He grinned. I grinned too for it did seem strange for two people to be so united, yet each to be unaware who the other was, and where he lived – a peculiar circumstance which was to recur later in my life. I tore a page out of my pocket book, halved it, and handed him one piece of the paper. He wrote his name, address and telephone number on it propped against the glazed door of the restaurant. He lent me his pencil, one of those cheap silver screw pencils with a cap and short india rubber on the end, with which I wrote on my half of the paper. It was rather dark on the pavement where we exchanged, as we supposed, our papers, and lingeringly clasped hands. 'It won't be longer than four days at the very most, I promise faithfully,' he said. 'Good! And here's your pencil,' I said, handing it back to him. 'No. Keep it. After all, what's mine is yours now,' was his reply. 'Righto! Then you must have this,' I said, offering him my old gunmetal Ingersoll watch, which was practically valueless, but

Though London is famous for the river which runs through its midst, there are today very few restaurants from which diners may obtain a view of the Thames from their tables. Perhaps there were more in 1862 when Richard Doyle the caricaturist depicted Dinner Down the River. *It must be admitted that only half a dozen of those present appear to be interested in the view, while the others are languidly enjoying their post-prandial drinks, smokes or snoozes. Coffee and candles are being brought in (left) to wake them out of their fish-like stupor.*

Dinner of the Dilettanti Society at the Thatched House Club. Victorian clubs and societies proliferated, meeting for elaborate dinners with a great variety of wines and spirits. Here a toast is being proposed. Note the imposing table decoration, the array of decanters and the wine cooler at right.

all I had. 'But you'll need it?' Theo asked. 'No, I won't; not till we meet again.' He took it. 'I'll love to have it – till we meet again then,' he repeated, adding, 'Next week, for sure,' and was off. For a second or two I watched him walk up Regent Street. Once he turned his head and smiled. Then I crossed the street, and striking up Piccadilly, walked all the way back to South Kensington.

I was in that seventh heaven in which, according to Mahomet, a man has 70,000 mouths, each with 70,000 tongues which in 70,000 languages chant the praises of the Most High. My gratitude found expression in soundless song. Here was someone who had come out of the blue to alter the whole course of my existence. I would conceivably be able to enrich his. What would we not mean to each other? What did we not mean already? I had long envied twin brothers who shared one mind, and in all other respects double capacities. And now I had found an even better substitute in someone whose greater intellect I respected. He too, thank goodness, was poor. In my pocket I tightly clutched, no longer my mother's crisp pound note but the precious bit of paper, the key to this new friendship.

It was long after midnight when I slipped through the door of No. 14 and crept upstairs to my room. I put the folded paper on the side-table, threw off my clothes and jumped into bed. What an evening I had had. What delicious extravagance. My first opera, first supper, and a new friend. Life did yield wonderful surprises. The future was bright indeed. Before turning out the light I would just see what Theo's surname was. I laughed. As though it really mattered. I picked up the paper and unfolded it. The writing on it seemed familiar. I was struck by a terrible foreboding. I read the words: Jim Lees-Milne, 14 Onslow Gardens, S.W.7. It was my handwriting. My paper. I was dumbfounded.

I never found Theo again. I racked my brain for ways of getting into touch with him. I searched every likely place. For weeks I used to wait outside the Opera House when performances were about to begin. I stood in the gallery the next time *Don Giovanni* was performed. I would hang around the entrance to the Café Royal, and wander upstairs scanning the tables. I have never so much as met anyone else called by his Christian name. I do not even know if it was the diminutive of Theodore (meaning God's gift), or Theophilus (the loved of God). Theobald and Theodoric seem less fitting. I often wonder if I shall read in *The Times* list of deaths the entry of someone exactly my age whose first name is Theo. Perhaps he was run over and killed on the way home the evening we parted. Perhaps he did not survive the war. Did he emigrate? Is he by now a venerable patriarch with a grey beard? A retired bank manager growing chrysanthemums at Southend-on-Sea? A lonely squire in Flintshire, who on winter evenings strums Mozart arias on an old Broadwood piano? Perhaps he was a seraph after all. I rather wish I knew. But I am not absolutely certain that I do.

I still have his pencil. It is a little tarnished now, and has a curiously old-fashioned look.

PRUE LEITH

Radis Beurre

The dish that made me into a cook was one that owes nothing whatever to cooking. It was a plate of *radis beurre* in a student restaurant in Paris. Of course students are always hungry so I guess the deliciousness of bread, butter and radishes might have been enhanced by this. Also, I was blessed with total ignorance in matters of gastronomy, so the dish was a revelation. I don't think I had ever eaten a radish in my life, having only seen them carved into hand-grenades and garnishing (horrible word) inedible food on buffet tables. But these radishes were not like that. First of all, they were tiny; secondly, they had white tips (I have since learnt they are called 'French Breakfast' in the seed catalogues and I have grown them every year, although without recapturing the taste of that canteen plateful of 1960); and, thirdly, they had their stalks and a few leaves intact. The *beurre* bit meant a large lump of unwrapped unsalted Normandy butter – real sweet butter, creamy and fresh: those were the days before EEC butter mountains.

Radis beurre lay in a refrigerated self-service cabinet along with other, to me, quite wonderful things: little glass bowls of grated carrot in French dressing; grated *raw* beetroot with lemon juice; skinned sliced tomatoes buried under chopped shallots. Everyone ate three courses. First: soup or crudités. Next: meat and potatoes or salad. Finally: little glass pots of plain yoghurt or

Artists found a ready market for certain genre paintings of dinners and these three, each by an artist born about the middle of the nineteenth century, are examples of a genre which hit the jackpot. Georges Croegaert (1) born in Antwerp, and François Brunery (3) born in Turin, were more successful than Adolf Humborg (2) born in Austria, though all three are still much in demand today by buyers in all parts of the world. Satirizing the excesses of the Roman Catholic Church, their success is perhaps explained by their appeal to the prevailing mood of anti-clericalism, as well as their sense of humour, as as in the Brunery which is entitled 'A la Santé de Son Eminence' with the pun on eminence.

Pheasants originated in Asia and were first introduced to Britain by the Romans as domestic fowl for the table; they all but vanished after the collapse of the Empire. Reintroduced by the Normans, they steadily became more popular as sporting quarry as the gun began to replace the falcon. Until the First World War the staple of English shooting was the partridge, long since overtaken by the the pheasant.

a piece of camembert or slice of chèvre. And the *bread*! You could kill for bread like that. The crust would crack and flake as the counterhand whacked the baguettes into foot-long pieces with her guillotine.

I watched the French students to see how to eat *radis beurre*: they mostly spread a bit of butter on a radish and ate it like that, followed by a bite of plain bread. But some put the butter, English fashion, on the bread, and made *le sandweech* with the radishes. Some dipped the radishes into the coarse salt pot on the formica tables. Over the next year I ate them all these ways, all equally good, and none equalled since.

I am sure Curnonsky was right: 'Cuisine is when things taste like what they are.'

MAUREEN LIPMAN

Is Something Wrong?

My most enduring restaurant memory is of a stony-faced American couple who ate a three-course meal in total silence in a West End bistro. Very occasionally she would sigh heavily. He would glance up, then quickly avert his eyes. Too quickly. Once or twice she, too, pointedly shifted her position between courses or studiously adjusted her make-up in a small gold hand-mirror. Once he put down his wine glass with unnecessary vigour and ground his crowns. The silence was more highly charged than the customers. Finally, it broke. Leaning tentatively across, he made some inaudible enquiry. She straightened her spine, placed her fork on her plate, fixed him with her astigmatism and growled with great deliberation, 'It's not the boeuf bourguinonne, Henry – it's the last twenty-three years!'

Gloire à Vénus, gloire à Bacchus by Frans Teichel. The connection between dining and amorous activities is a long one, stretching back well before the Roman preoccupation with the aphrodisiacal qualities of certain foods. Here is a nineteenth-century German romantic view, with the men as harlequins and the women wearing trousers.

One of the most famous dinners to end in dalliance was the one enjoyed by Tom Jones and the fetching Mrs Walters. Fielding describes how at first Jones's appetite was for the food. 'The god of eating (if there be any such deity, for I do not confidently assert it) preserved his votary . . . for as love frequently preserves from the attacks of hunger, so may hunger possibly, in some cases, defend us against love.' Before long, however, Jones's defences are down 'and the fair conqueror enjoyed the usual fruits of her victory.'

ELIZABETH LONGFORD

Waiter, There's a Rhyme in My Soup

It was a super grand dinner and we were preparing to enjoy our exquisite clear soup, served in golden soup plates by white-gloved footmen. Suddenly, from the gilded ceiling far above our heads descended something like a tiny silent bomb and plummetted into my soup. A dead bluebottle. What had dislodged it at that moment from the richly carved rafters? Perhaps the vibrations of the band, or the loud burst of conversation after Grace. The white-gloved footman stared at my plate in disbelief, changing to horror. Snatching the plate away, he promised to bring me some more. He never did. I felt somehow guilty. The perfect guest would surely have swallowed the bluebottle as silently as it had arrived, just as one successful candidate for a fellowship at All Souls College, Oxford, was said to have swallowed his cherry stones rather than spit them out. But then I remembered the nursery rhyme and was glad I had not tried to be too ladylike:

> There was an old lady who swallowed a fly,
> Poor old lady, she's sure to die.
> There was an old lady who swallowed a cow,
> I don't know how she swallowed a cow.
> There was an old lady who swallowed a horse,
> She died of course.

DAME VERA LYNN

We'll Meet Again

One particular dinner that stays in my memory was the one the Variety Club International gave for me in Israel. It was when they presented to me the 1984 International Humanitarian Award for my various works for charity. I had, of course, to sing for

Cobbett, in his Rural Rides, *wrote: 'I saw, and with great delight, a pig at almost every labourer's house.' Bacon in its various forms was the principal meat course at working-class dinners in the nineteenth century, as it had been in earlier years. As agriculture declined, so the rural workforce found it harder to make ends meet, particularly when imports affected the price they could obtain for their produce at market. They had less and less money to buy food and as the child of a farm labourer lamented 'we never had butcher's meat.' Tea was the main drink, beer being too expensive except for celebrations.*

PUNCH, OR THE LONDON CHARIVARI.—September 19, 1863.

THE PIG AND THE PEASANT.

Peasant "Ah! I'd like to be cared vor half as well as thee be!"

my supper; and it was very moving for me to have a group of Israeli children singing with me 'We'll Meet Again'. They showed films and videos of various incidents of my career.

The guests of the evening included President Hertzog and Prime Minister Shimon Perez. The latter gave a wonderful speech which pointed out that millions are killed in war but each one is an individual. Variety Club helps millions of children, and again each one is an individual, one by one, by one, by one, by one.

BERNARD LEVIN

If Music Be the Food of Love, It's Just as Well

The publication of my long (and eagerly) awaited definitive study, *The Art of Picknicking at Glyndebourne* (OUP, 8 vols, illus.), has, I regret to say, once more been postponed, this time to await the findings of the exhaustive investigation undertaken by the Physics Department of Sussex University (with the aid of a generous grant from MacFisheries Ltd, which has made possible the purchase of the most modern sonar equipment) in an attempt to settle once and for all the age-old riddle of whether there are or are not smoked trout in the lake. I have therefore been prevailed upon to provide the following, necessarily abbreviated, general conspectus of the subject; I must emphasize that it constitutes the merest glance over the vast territory, and is in no way to be considered a digest of the principal work. I take the liberty of dedicating it to the memory of Dr August Katzenbalgerei of Göttingen University, my chief research assistant, whose promising career was so tragically cut short last summer when he choked to death on a portion of *quiche lorraine* in the course of a series of field studies.

I must begin by pointing out, though many will consider it heresy, if not indeed blasphemy, to do so, that in most respects picnicking at Glyndebourne is no different from picnicking elsewhere. The most important of these common elements is the fact that it is not possible to be comfortable while picnicking, for a number of elementary physiological reasons. Until the human body comes equipped with legs fully detachable at the hip (patrons of the Royal Festival Hall will be aware that the distance between the rows of seats there was apparently determined on the premature assumption that this startling evolutionary development had already taken place) there is no position it can adopt which can be held for more than a very few minutes at a time without becoming insupportably painful. If, for instance, the back is kept perpendicular, then either the legs must be stuck out in front with the knees drawn up somewhat – a position which entails the constant danger of involuntarily kicking out, under the sudden onset of an attack of cramp, thus upsetting the wine into the sandwiches, and which in any case puts an unbearable strain on the spine – or the picnicker must sit cross-legged, which not only puts an even greater strain on the spine but which speedily results in all sensation in the legs being lost, in some cases permanently. If, on the other hand,

The nineteenth century saw immense changes in British dining arrangements. In 1801 only one fifth of the population lived in towns – most were rural; by 1851 the proportions were evenly balanced; but soon after the turn of the century they were reversed with four fifths of the population in towns and cities. This couple – drawn by Charles Keene (1823–91) – would probably not have seen a sizeable town if they had been members of the great farming population, but now as town-dwellers they could afford to dine in a chop-house. By the following century, couples like this were dining at home, alone, a novel experience after centuries of communal eating.

Richard Doyle the cartoonist expressed his idea of farmers in this 1849 sketch, made at the end of the Hungry Forties, as they came to be called. The misery of the British farm labourers has been described by a historian of food as representing 'a population existing on the edge of starvation.' The Irish – Ireland then being a part of Great Britain – suffered exceptionally badly. Thousands emigrated to America and others came to the towns which adapted themselves from a market-based commerce to one where food was supplied by shops. Note, by the way, the pineapples on the table. A Punch cartoon asked how to cook them.

the picnicker adopts the horizontal mode, resting on one elbow and stretched out parallel to the edge of the food area, dislocation of the lower shoulder is almost inevitable, and that is quite apart from the additional strain of trying to decide whether to hold the sandwich in the hand which is attached to the grounded limb, thus dangerously reducing the freedom of manoeuvre to the small arc describable by the forearm, or in the upper, free-range, hand, thus risking, in the event of only a minor wobble by the pivoting elbow, a cup of coffee down the bosom. (At the cost of being thought digressive, I must here mention the occasion when, having a leisurely lunch on the way to Glyndebourne from London, I ended the meal by depositing about a tablespoonful of raspberry sorbet on the front of my dress shirt, and had to stop in East Grinstead to get a replacement. I entered the main gentlemen's outfitters and strode up to the counter saying 'As you can see, I have recently committed a murder, and wish to buy a shirt, so that I may get rid of the traces.' Either the assistant didn't believe me, or homicide is rather more frequent in that part of Sussex than I had supposed, for all he said was 'What size collar, sir?') The two methods are clearly demonstrated in Manet's *Déjeuner sur l'herbe*; the lady in the foreground, who so scandalized Paris in 1863 by her costume, which could not be said to be evening dress even in the widest definition of Glyndebourne's 'informal', has adopted the upright-back position, while the gentleman with the hat and the beard favours the elbow-pivot. Both will be sorry in the morning.

Nor are matters much improved by those who attempt to solve the problem by bringing collapsible tables and chairs. In the first place, as Pythagoras's Other Theorem demonstrates, no picnic table is ever at the right height for any picnic chair, or *vice versa*. In the second place, any collapsible piece of furniture will, sooner or later, unexpectedly collapse; I need not dwell on the range of possible consequences, except to reveal that

in the Black Museum at Glyndebourne (which is situated beyond the mysterious locked door in the corner of the Organ Room) there is one showcase entirely devoted to a display of thumbs, all of which have been abruptly severed in this manner.

Let us suppose, however, that the physical problems of picnicking (and there are many others, including the selection of a suitable site – a quest which has led to many an unseemly wrangle and on one occasion to the pushing of an elderly Peer of the Realm into the ha-ha) have been solved. The picnic party is still faced with the far greater variety of problems that the selection of food presents. One of the greatest fallacies in this particular field of human conduct is the belief that sandwiches tend to get dry and to curl up at the edges. I have reason to suppose that this myth originated with the sandwiches to be found at British Rail buffets, of which it is undoubtedly true – indeed, a standing instruction to the staff of those places obliges them to hose the dreadful things down twice a week. But that is because the plastic of which British Rail sandwiches are made is of an unstable type which tends to wilt; sandwiches composed of food have the opposite tendency altogether – that is, to become squashed and limp during the drive down and Act One, not brittle. (The problem is much accentuated in the case of sandwiches made with egg mayonnaise, and an additional threat is posed by beetroot, which not only registers exceptionally high scores on my Sogginess Quotient Index, but is capable of staining everything else in the hamper through three thicknesses of kitchen foil.)

Many wise picnickers therefore eschew sandwiches altogether, though in doing so they only escape from one set of problems into another, chief of those faced by the no-sandwich school being the Cutlery Question. Chicken legs and lamb cutlets can be eaten with the fingers, though to my taste cold cutlets are insipid, and the fact that there are only two legs to a chicken

Francis Rawdon-Hastings, 2nd Earl of Moira and Governor-General of India, and his Countess being entertained by the Nawab Wazir Ghazi-ud-din in Lucknow, the capital of the province of Oudh, in about 1814. There is no concession to Western eating habits – the Nawab reaches among the welter of cups and dishes for the initial titbit, the eating of which will, like a pistol-shot at a race, signal the beginning of the feast. Moira must have been impressed, for he made the Nawab 'King' of Oudh in 1819.

The Prince Regent hosted a splendid English version of a French dinner at the Brighton Pavilion on 15 January 1817, masterminded by the first of the great French chefs, Antonin Carême. There were four soups, four fish dishes, four grosses pièces *(ham, goose, chicken and veal) flanked by thirty-six* entrées *of both fish and meat, as well as game birds. There were in addition five* assiettes volantes *of fillets of sole and five of hazel grouse. Afterwards eight great set-pieces made of sugar icing were brought in, designed to be looked at. Then there were four roasts of game or poultry and thirty-two* entremets. *Then another ten* assiettes volantes. *It was all too much and no guest could possibly taste everything. The extensive kitchens, pictured here, may still be visited.*

(breeders are working on that problem) means an exceptionally high wastage-rate; but as soon as anything more ambitious, even a slice of game pie, is included, knives and forks have to be included too. There is nothing wrong with knives and forks, except that knives and forks mean plates, and plates (because you cannot balance a plate on your knees if you intend to ply eating-irons on its surface) entail trays, and in the end you have to bring a hamper so large that you risk having it commandeered by the producer for use in Act Two of *Falstaff*. Moreover, if you return, in the face of this problem, to the cutlets-and-chicken-legs menu, you immediately face the necessity of cleaning the fingers at the end of the meal, as you would have to be remarkably nimble, not to say eccentric, to picnic in gloves. To this problem, as a matter of fact, there is an infallible solution; an ample supply of those little cologne-impregnated tissues in sachets. (During a performance on a very hot night a few years ago, the wife of the gentleman sitting beside me became faint, and I was happily able to come to the rescue by passing him a couple of these useful items which, dabbed on the forehead and the back of the neck, provide an admirable substitute for smelling-salts. I mention this episode not to boast about my presence of mind, but to record the most scrupulous and delicate act of *gentillesse* I have ever come across; I ran into the same couple at Glyndebourne again a few weeks later, and he, with a courteous bow, insisted on paying me back the two sachets.)

Keeping the drink cold is another problem the picnicker faces. Those zip-up cold-bags provide the obvious solution, but there is a catch in them; they are apt to reduce the temperature of the wine to a point approaching Absolute Zero, though one intrepid Glyndebourne reveller I heard about, faced by the discovery that the contents of his bottle had frozen solid, nonchalantly smashed it against a fence-post and was to be seen happily sucking the only hock-lolly in history. Many Glyndebourne picnickers favour tying one end of a piece of string round the neck of the bottle and the other end round a lakeside tree and throwing the tethered bottle into the water, to be reclaimed at interval-time; the only snag here is that, with the general national decline in moral standards having now affected even opera-goers, there have been cases of frogmen creeping along beneath the surface and severing the lines, though I treat with some reserve the report that in one case of such banditry the robber went so far as to replace a magnum of exceptionally fine Sancerre Clos de la Poussie with a bottle of Mackeson's Stout, and an empty one at that.

Of course, just as Glyndebourne is an exceptionally pleasant place to hear opera, so it is an exceptionally pleasant place to picnic, and I dare say this world provides few delights to compare with watching the sun begin to go down over Mr Christie's demesnes at the end of a well-ordered *alfresco* meal which is itself an interlude between the two halves of an evening of Mozart. Mind you, I must here reveal that one of the pleasantest elements in the feeling thus produced is not natural, but devised by Mr Christie for the further delectation of his guests. If you look up at the hillside beyond the car park (itself, of course, invisible to the picnicker), you will see the sheep quietly grazing. Now, some years ago, I was struck by the realization that although these amiable beasts moved back and forth laterally along the contours, they never turned up or down the hill, and this ultimately led me, after many seasons studying them with powerful binoculars, to the astounding discovery that they are not real sheep at all, but exceptionally lifelike cut-out models, made of wood and drawn along grooves in the ground by an ingenious arrangement of wires; this whole *mise-en-scène* was designed by Mr Oliver Messel, and in my opinion is one of his finest achievements, surpassed only by his unforgettable designs for *Die Entführung*.

LEO McKERN

You Vill Enchoy It!

During the making of the film *Help!* we were cut off for days at the location in the Tyrol, which affected the shooting not at all, although the results of the day's filming had to be flown out by helicopter for processing. We were accommodated in various hotels, and our family shared one with John Bluthal, and meal-times there turned out to be somewhat hysterical. Our waiter was an almost unbelievable living caricature, reminding us instantly of Ronnie Barker's Teutonic travel agent. . . . 'You vill *enchoy* your holiday in Chermany! If you do not, ve haf vays off *makink* you enchoy it!' A typical conversation at dinner would go something like this:

'You are ready to order?'
'Ah, yes . . . I'll have the melon to start . . .'
'Strawberries.'
'No, not strawberries . . . the melon.'
'Strawberries are to be preferred.'
'Yes, I daresay, but I'd rath . . .'
'Viz cream?'
'No, not with melon, thank y . . .'
'Gut! *Strawberries* mit *cream!*'
'But I prefer the . . .'
'*Alpine* strawberries!'
'Oh, for G . . . Yes, all right, strawberries . . . and a Schnitzel to follo . . .'

Guildhall Banquet after the Great Reform Bill *by Benjamin Robert Haydon. The First Reform Act of June 1832 removed some of the more glaring anomalies in the British Parliamentary system – such as 'rotten' and 'pocket' boroughs; the overall effect in England, however, was to enfranchise the upper-middle classes. When Wellington saw the first Reformed Parliament, he remarked that 'I never saw so many shocking bad hats in all my life.' The Reverend Sydney Smith, on the other hand, was an ardent supporter of reform, which he eulogized with his customary – and famous – wit: 'There will be mistakes at first as there are in all changes. All young Ladies will imagine that they will be instantly married. Schoolboys believe gerunds and supines will be abolished and that currant tarts must come down in price; the corporal is sure of double pay; bad poets will expect a demand for their epics; reasonable men will find that a very serious good has been obtained.' There are pineapples on the table (indeed, the gentleman at bottom far left is holding one, looking rather as though he is wondering whether he dare steal it), which would still then have been something of a novelty. Evelyn's Diary mentions a pineapple at the table of Charles II, thought to be the first mention of the fruit in English literature; a native of tropical America, the pineapple was first cultivated in England in 1712.*

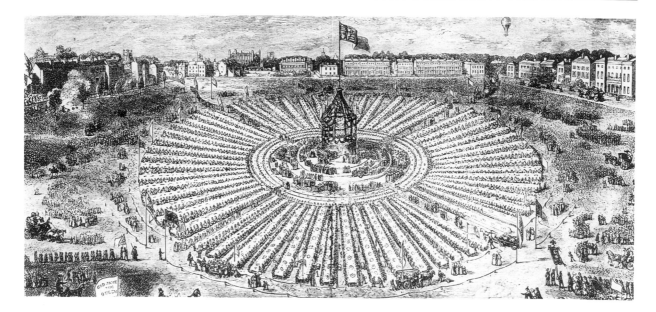

'No.'

'What?'

'No.You vill haf die Forelle . . . vat you say . . . trout!'

'But I don't want trout! I want the Sch . . .'

'Mit der chef's special sause! . . . delicious!'

'But I . . .'

'Und sauté potatoes und Salat!'

'I had the bloo . . . I had trout last night! . . . tonight I want the Sch . . .'

'I vill myself take it from ze bone . . . you vill zank me you have it!'

'Look, just bring me a Schn . . .'

'Und zer *incredible* Pleck Forest Gateau!'

'*No sweet*, thank you! . . . just coffee.'

'Mit *vipped* cream!'

'Just milk.'

'*Milk!* Mit Pleck Forest Gateau?'

A 'Grand Coronation Fête' held on Parker's Piece, Cambridge, on 28 June 1838, the day Queen Victoria was crowned — she was a month past her nineteenth birthday, and would reign for another 64 years, dying a few months short of her eighty-second birthday. Anyone who knows Parker's Piece will be more than a little surprised that it could hold such an apparently vast multitude; but it may be that the artist's loyal sentiments got the better of his sense of perspective.

Equally, it is difficult to know where in Stratford-upon-Avon there might have been erected a pavilion vast enough to hold the diners commemorating Shakespeare's 300th birthday in April 1864. Here the 7th Earl of Carlisle proposes the toast to 'The Memory of Shakespeare'. Carlisle, Lord Lieutenant of Ireland, besides being a politican, was an ardent supporter of the reformation of juvenile criminals, and a cultured and cultivated man who outlived this banquet by only eight months.

Pure Love

This engraving, from a painting by William Salter, depicts one of the Waterloo Banquets, held in Apsley House on 18 June 1836. Most of the guests would have been survivors from among Wellington's officers: by the 1830s many of them had become generals. Wellington is addressing the guests. On the table is the Portuguese silver centre-piece, given to the Duke in appreciation of his liberation of Portugal and still in Apsley House.

A rather unconventional dinner was held in a large rehearsal room at the National Theatre, on the eve of Bob Hoskin's marriage, during the run of *Guys and Dolls*.

An elaborate ruse had been planned by Richard Gere to keep the Hoskins off the scent and, at eleven o'clock, Bill Paterson, in full Highland gear, piped them into the room, which had been transformed into a nightclub with candles, tables with floor-length cloths, and a cabaret especially written for them by members of the company. They enjoyed poached salmon (prepared by me) and champagne. The whole event was done with enormous affection for them – I know they loved it – and it remains the highlight of my party-going experiences, simply because it was all done with pure love.

SPIKE MILLIGAN

A Farewell Dinner

In Poona's main street was an Italian restaurant, Muratores; it was there the Sparrows [the Milligans] decided to have the farewell dinner. They invited Bombardier Eggit and his soppy wife Emily. The ladies dressed up for the evening and the men wore best dress.

'Oh, this is posh,' said Emily as they entered Muratores.

It was a big stone-flagged room with several punkahs. Tables had starched white cloths, napery, vases of flowers and lots of potted ferns. Uniformed turbanned waiters stood in attendance, an effusive Mr Muratore greeted them.

'Good-a-evenings, Mr Sparrow,' he smiled. 'I no see you for a longa time.'

'What a coincidence,' said Leo. 'I haven't seen you for a long time either.'

Mr Muratore, full of Italian volubility and garlic, ushered them to their table. 'Please-a-please, sitt-tit-a down. Gopal,' he beckoned a waiter, waving his arms like a policeman at a traffic junction. 'Now-a-we hav-a esssspecial men-a-u: fresh prauns [prawns] with-a-new pititoes [potatoes] garlic bride [bread] timitoes [tomatoes] Brussels-a-sprites [sprouts],' as he spoke he made great theatrical gestures, and there was a grand finale as he announced, 'hend the ipple [apple] pie!!!' They all applauded his efforts.

'Very nice,' said Leo. 'Now can we have something to eat.'

Perusing a menu Florence said, 'What's the chicken like?'

Mr Muratore shrugged his shoulder. 'It doesn't like anything, it's dead.'

Eggit waved some flies off his face, 'My God, these flies are on everything.'

'Especially you,' said Leo and laughed. A fly flew into his mouth, he was seized with a spit-spluttering cough. 'Blast, I

The Unlicensed Victuallers' Dinner by George Cruikshank (1798–1878). There have always been some who have attacked the consumption of alcohol at meal times, and Cruikshank was prouder of his efforts to preach temperance than he was of any of his other artistic work. His pictures included 'The Gin Bottle', 'The Gin Trap', 'The Gin Juggernaut' and 'The Drunkard's Children', as well as this print of 1841 in which he tried to kill two birds with one stone by attacking the brewers themselves. Though the diners are not drinking, the names of many brewers still famous today are recognizable on the wall, behind their groaning table covered with public-house viands.

Opening of the new Metropolitan Meat Market in Smithfield, in December 1868. The Victorian vogue for old English customs had its effect on food: many English culinary 'traditions' were reinvented in the nineteenth century. A boar's head is being carved on the left: the custom of serving this as a Christmas dish is said to derive from Norse mythology. Freyr, the god of peace and plenty, used to ride around on a boar, and at Yuletide, a boar was sacrificed in his honour. At the Smithfield dinner, the guests 'notwithstanding the abundance of viands on the table', kept the carvers busy until four barons of beef and as many boars' heads had been consumed. The term 'baron' of beef is jocosely said to be a pun on 'sirloin'.

swallowed the blasted thing.'

'I hope they don't charge us for it,' said Florence, banging Leo on his back.

'Have a glass of water,' she said.

'What good will that do?' said Leo.

'It will drown it,' said Florence.

'Quick, a glass of Catalan wine, there's some in the Gibraltar!'

The fly incident over, they ordered chicken madras and an omelette for Emily – all the way to India to order an omelette!

'We'll miss you when you're gone,' said Eggit and his flies. 'What will we do for entertainment?'

'Nobody's indispensable,' said Leo and his flies.

Emily added wit and sparkle to the conversation. 'This omelette is very nice,' she said.

'I'm so glad to hear that,' said Leo. 'Aren't you, Flo?'

'Is everything orl rite-a,' said Mr Muratore in fluent broken English.

'Yes, thank you,' said Leo.

'The omelette is very nice,' said Emily.

Muratore's face lit up and then went out, 'Would-a you like-a drink on-a the house,' he said.

'We'd rather have it down here,' said Leo. There was no cure for him.

'Excuse, please? said Mr Muratore.

'Don't listen to him, Mr Muratore,' said Florence. So Mr Muratore didn't listen to him. He returned with four glasses of Moët & Chandon, which the diners greeted with ooos and ahhhs.

ROGER MOATE MP

If . . .

In the course of my work, I attend many formal dinners, but I am pleased to say that I have never had to adopt the formula used by one practised after-dinner speaker. When asked if he had enjoyed his meal, he gave this candid reply:

> If the soup had been as warm as the wine,
> And if the wine had been as old as the chicken
> And if the chicken had been as plump and as tender
>   as the waitress,
> And if she had been as willing as the elderly dowager
>   sitting next to me,
> Then it would have been an excellent meal.

BOB MONKHOUSE

Waving, Not Drowning

My Most Memorable Experience While Eating Dinner happened in Barbados about four years ago. Our friends, Mike and Lynn Pemberton, have two hotels side by side on the beach at St James, Glitter Bay and the Royal Pavilion. Next to them is their private house, Bachelor Hall. Its terrace runs out onto the beach where a former owner extended it out towards the gentle Caribbean with a kind of coral stone stage.

This platform on the sand is a perfect setting for a moonlit dinner and, one evening, when the wind was gently warm and the soft little waves were lapping, we strolled with our glasses of Dom Pérignon through the gardens with other laughing guests to take our places at the beautiful dinner-table under the stars.

The Pembertons' gifted chef and his staff served a wonderful, wonderful dinner. Beluga caviare and blintzes. Barbados

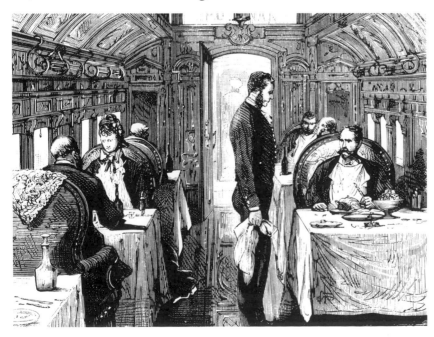

A Pullman dining car on the Great Northern Railway, 1879. Dining on the train is always something of a luxury, though it was the arrival of the railways in the 1830s that changed the dining habits of the whole nation in a different sense — by bringing about a revolution in the supply of food to the towns. Soon, fish caught on the east coast in the morning was arriving in Birmingham the same evening and diners in London could have Scottish salmon, packed in ice, at all seasons. The railways cut costs as well as time.

Mr Pickwick addresses his friends *by Charles Green (1840–98). Dickens describes how Pickwick and his friends dined at five, starting with fish, continuing with broiled fowl and mushrooms, washed down with plenty of wine. The stranger who was present described a dining custom which survives to this day in the tradition of passing the port to the left. 'Beg your pardon, sir,' he said to Pickwick, 'bottle stands – pass it round – way of the sun – through the button-hole – no heel taps.'*

pumpkin bisque and banana bread. Pan-fried flying fish and white grapes with a 1979 Jadot Bâtard-Montrachet. Châteaubriands and a macédoine of local vegetables with a 1976 Marc Doudet Moulin à Vent. Then came the crêpes Véronique with a 1950 Château d'Yquem. The butler was just serving the port, a magnificent 1963 Fonseca, when it happened.

There is a very rare tidal effect in the Caribbean Sea which I believe is called a Columbine. Apparently it occurs when a very large number of small waves coincide with each other in an overlapping formation to become one very big wave. I've only seen it once. Correction – I've never actually *seen* it, just experienced it. I was sitting with my back to it.

The guests facing me and the sea watched it coming. They didn't believe their eyes, which I saw widen. All I knew about it before it hit was the noise of a London bus being driven down Ben Nevis and, as I prepared to turn to look at this uncommon sight, the Superwave struck.

Reports afterwards about the height of the thing varied a bit. Some said one mile high, others said two miles. Not having seen it, only felt it, I'd say it was the same kind of natural phenomenon that destroyed Atlantis.

My wife and I visit Barbados every year and now we've actually built a home there, our own little sandcastle on the beach, the very same beach at St James that witnessed the drowning

OLD TOM TOWLER.

of the dinner-party. We plan to live there for part of each year that is left to us. And to make sure as many years as possible are left to us, we're not planning to eat anything with our backs to the water.

LORD MONTAGU OF BEAULIEU

A Moving Recollection

The annual dinner of the First Guards Club, the senior dining club of the Grenadier Guards, is always a memorable affair, but I recall one in particular.

Our guest of honour was an old Grenadier, Harold Macmillan, who after dinner rose to his feet and, starting very quietly, proceeded to give us up to an hour's talk on the horrors of the First World War. It was a very moving occasion and I always regret that it was not recorded, as he spoke representing a generation of young men, the majority of whom were wiped out in the trenches in France. He also spoke of the tragedies of the post-war depression and how many of the survivors failed to settle down and get good jobs after the war, leading to the great Jarrow Marches of the thirties.

At the end of the dinner most people did not feel like applauding, although of course we did.

Hunting dinners and, even more, hunting breakfasts litter the pages of Surtees. Here John Leech portrays Tom Towler, the huntsman, looking less impressive off a horse, making a late arrival to discuss the day's sport.

ROBERT MORLEY

Noël or Nothing

I have been known to disregard the cutlet and confine myself to the aspic. Sometimes my hostess has proved to be as unpredictable as my table manners.

What was I to make of Dorothy Paget, who, after my performance, would begin hers in the Rolls-Royce which was to take us to dine? On occasion, for an hour or so at a time, we would be confined to her motor, anchored outside her front door while the caviare warmed and the goose waned and she expounded her theories of horse-breeding.

Then too there was the night she took me to the Café de Paris to hear Noël Coward, who, to my certain knowledge, had concluded his season a month earlier. I was prepared for her disappointment when she summoned the Maître and asked if he could persuade Mr Coward to postpone his performance for half an hour or so.

'I do not care to be sung to while I am eating,' Miss Paget explained. She was a diabetic with a prodigious appetite.

'That will be easy, Miss Paget,' the head waiter replied, 'Mr Coward is no longer with us.'

'Whom have you got?' she asked, and on being informed who was to take his place opined that as she had never heard of him, his fee should be placed on her bill and his services dispensed with. She was reminded that she was by no means the sole patron of the restaurant.

'Well,' she commanded, 'tell him to delay until I have finished the lobster and we'll be off.'

JAN MORRIS

The Best Meal in the World

Long ago I identified the Best Meal in the World – the best meal, that is, of the kind that restaurant guides like to call an *experience*, or even a *happening*. Having enjoyed over the years a succession of meals which I wrongly thought were the best imaginable, I tracked it down definitively to Stockholm, Sweden, on a Sunday shortly before Christmas. It is a smorgasbord, the most famous of all the world's smorgasbords in fact, as served at the most celebrated of Sweden's restaurants, the Operakallaren on the ground floor of the Royal Opera House.

They serve it there every day, but Sunday is the best day because then, by a long-established custom, Stockholmers like to go there *en famille*: and a Sunday shortly before Christmas is best of all, for under the blessing of St Lucia one may then share the pleasures of the Swedes at their most genial, their most generous and (I choose my words carefully, for they are an abstemious people) their least ungluttonous. So I enjoyed it myself, on a Christmassy Stockholm Sunday of the 1980s.

The ambience of the meal was tremendous. The great baroque dining-room is decorated with a series of mythological paintings which were thought in the 1890s to be downright indecent, but now just seem amiably nubile, and it looks out through big windows to the harbour and the palace. On that Sunday

the victuals were displayed on a gigantic table in the middle, and above them, just for Christmas, was suspended a large gingerbread model of the Opera House itself. The light of the chandeliers was subdued, the warmth was palpable, the head waiter who showed me so courteously to my table looked like a Baltic duke.

White, white was my table-cloth, velvety my chair, fastidiously polished the cutlery, and before I got any further here before me was my glass of the Operakallaren's own aquavit, Stenborgare, named after an eighteenth-century opera singer, subtly flavoured with fennel and aniseed, and available nowhere else. *Skoll!* Like aromatic fire it went down, and I was ready in body and spirit for The Best Meal in the World.

It was a feast of feasts, not only of food, but of life and sociability too. The Swedes are famously reserved, but once their shyness is broached they are the most companionable of people, and as I lined up plate in hand for nourishment kindly voices guided me towards the most interesting pickled herrings, explained to me the history of Stenborgare, introduced me to their mother-in-law Mrs Andersson, or abjured little Erik to stand up straight when addressing strangers.

Little Erik, actually, was standing up admirably straight already, dressed as he was in his best suit, with a bow tie and a rather uncomfortable collar, and his sister Eva was extremely smart in blue check, and Mrs Andersson was a most elegant old dame, and altogether my companions presented a splendid picture of plump well-being and goodwill, as they urged me to shovel another portion of elk-meat on to the corner of my plate.

Elk-meat, or Swedish caviare, or salmon from great ravaged carcasses, or game, or berries, or cheeses, or cream, or prawns,

Disraeli described his Two Nations *in 1845 as formed by a different breeding, fed by a different food and ordered by different manners. Yet the eating habits of the 'rich' were changing too, partly because there were more of them, and many more people now had servants. This Pears' soap print is clearly a nostalgic backward look to that most memorable of all dinners, Christmas, in the days when the traditional food of Olde England reigned supreme.*

or pickles, or reindeer tongue – 'you can always come back for more,' said Mrs Andersson encouragingly. I took her advice, too, for the afternoon was long, another Stenborgare presently turned up from nowhere, and the conversation was delightfully digestive. 'Will you not have some cloudberries?' asked Eva in her most careful English, 'people like them very much in Sweden.' And I did, I did.

So the hours passed, and soon it was pitch dark outside the windows, and the lights of the flambeaux were dancing and flickering in the dark. As soon as one family of Anderssons left, another, just as well-dressed, just as smiling, was shown to its table. One salmon was replaced by the next on the great smorgasbord table, elk succeeded elk, shoals of herrings came and went. The head waiter, when at last the time came for me to leave, no longer seemed like a head waiter at all, or even a duke, but more like an old family friend. I said goodbye to him almost nostalgically: by the nature of things, The Best Meal in the World can come but once a year.

JOHN MORTIMER

Memory Bites

I don't know if the 'marriage ending' cards were dealt when we first stood on the beach in Ireland and Penelope was overcome with thoughts of death. Perhaps the course was set as we grew up far apart, in a faithless lawyer's garden and a sceptical parson's vicarage. At any rate the time had come to do what I had done for so many other people and plan a divorce. I remember a meeting we had, a meal in the Rose Garden at Regent's Park, to discuss the depressing details, the sorting out of money, the allocation of books and pictures, which go with funerals and the formal ending of a marriage.

I had had a minor dental disaster that morning, a part of the facade of a cap had come adrift and I went to have it stuck on again. My dentist at that time was a cheerful Australian who had a surgery complete with nurses in white mini-skirts, Vivaldi tapes and a pattern of coloured lights to keep you entertained while in the chair. Later my dentist disappeared in a mysterious fashion but that, as they say, is another story. I emerged from the 'Son et Lumière' with my tooth repaired to keep my open-air luncheon appointment with the wife who had once helped me by typing out my divorce petitions. She came to the Rose Garden Restaurant with her dog and put the lead and her packet of cigarettes and her lighter on the table. We sat in the sunshine and Penelope ordered spare-ribs. It was extraordinarily peaceful as we sat surrounded by a silence which was only emphasized by the distant murmur of traffic. We talked, in perfect friendliness, and discussed our plans for the future. I remembered staying with her parents at the vicarage, the huge family meals, the feeling of daring and excitement as I left the scene of my lonely childhood and joined what seemed like a great colony of people whom I had later seen grow up and leave to live their separate lives. I remembered the places we had visited, the houses we had taken, the years we had spent writing and reading each other's words, waiting, in terrible suspense,

The revolution in middle- and upper-class dining habits which occurred in the mid-nineteenth century was one of timing. In the eighteenth century and earlier there had been breakfast, a midday meal (dinner) and a lightish supper. Now, social mores called for a large dinner in the evening, at eight o'clock or even later, and this required a rearrangement of other meals. Breakfast came earlier, and it might almost be said that the early Victorian age invented luncheon as a third meal of the day. This word itself had an uncertain history, with Dr Johnson defining 'nunchin' as 'a piece of victuals eaten between meals'. Here a débutante of 1890 describes the picture as 'A dinner party during my first season' probably beginning about eight. The array of cutlery on the table suggests that they are in for a long evening.

A débutante was a well-born girl making her 'début' in Society; her first season was that in which she first put her hair up; first attended all the society functions of 'the Season'; and was presented to the monarch. The system was, in truth, a form of marriage market.

for each other's smallest sign of approval. As we talked Penelope lifted a spare-rib and bit into it.

Suddenly, and it was like a frozen frame in a movie, my wife sat, spare-rib in hand, immobilized and with a look of horror. Then the film moved on again. She gathered up her dog, her cigarettes and her lighter and, without a word of explanation, she was gone from the park.

I sat on at the table, half expecting her to return. I had a feeling of being suspended and lost in time. I might sit there, perhaps forever, and that table in that place might be the end of a journey and I would have to go no further. Or I could walk away from Regent's Park into a new life and leave the Law Courts and the rehearsal rooms forever.

Thinking all these things I lifted the half-eaten spare-rib from Penelope's plate and bit into it. I felt a slight pull on a gum and then I realized that something was missing from my mouth. My exotic dentist had been too distracted by the mini-skirts or the subliminal Vivaldi to fix the broken section of the cap on properly.

Before I had time to consider the full implications of the loss, the waitress said there was a telephone call for me. I went, puzzled, into the shadows of the restaurant, lifted the receiver and heard from Penelope who had just reached her house. She said she was sorry she had left so abruptly. I said that I understood perfectly and that it was not an easy thing for anyone to sit at a meal discussing a divorce. It wasn't that exactly, she explained. What had happened was that, as she bit into her

A Midi chez Bignon, 1884
*by Antoine Druet. One reason
for the new 'dinner' time was
that the breadwinner of the
rising and expanding middle
class moved his family out
into the suburbs, so he would
probably have lunch in his
club instead of his home. His
wife would make do with a
light meal at midday – thus
luncheon became an invention
of ladies of leisure. However,
some men did not like the
concept of a long lunch –
Macaulay, for example,
complained bitterly in 1853 of
the need to break into the
working day in order to eat.
A further development was
the invention of afternoon tea.*

spare-rib, a cap came off her tooth and she didn't want to go on sitting with a mouth full of gap. Again I understood entirely and said we'd meet again soon, wouldn't we?

I went out into the sunshine where the plates hadn't yet been cleared away. And there was the spare-rib which had captured fragments of dentistry from each of us and which held them tightly and remorselessly together.

ANTON MOSIMANN

Homage to a Great Conductor

It was a great honour to be invited to Sir Georg Solti's seventy-fifth birthday dinner. There were about twenty people at their London home, including Mr and Mrs Thatcher. Although I have cooked for the former Prime Minister many times, including at Number 10 Downing Street when she was in office, this was the first occasion that we were fellow diners.

I admire Sir Georg greatly; although a Hungarian, he has very close associations with Switzerland. The evening reflected his love of my home country, indeed the menu did too, as the main course was Veal Zürich style served with Roesti.

It is amazing to think that Sir Georg, at 75, is still one of the most revered conductors and is in demand with all the famous orchestras throughout the world. Indeed his recent Channel 4 series, in which he, together with Dudley Moore, explored various musical instruments, did much to popularize something that was once considered élitist.

The evening was a tremendous success and one I look back to with fond memories and great affection for both Sir Georg and Lady Solti.

Name-Dropping

In the mid-1970s I was visiting Canada in my capacity as Colonel-in-Chief of Princess Patricia's Canadian Light Infantry. My father, Earl Mountbatten of Burma, and I were travelling together as he was fulfilling engagements of his own. We arrived to stay at a small Government House with a very new, and therefore rather nervous, Provincial Lieutenant-Governor who had only been in office for one week. He and his wife had arranged a dinner party for us which turned out to be a very enjoyable and friendly affair, but with some speeches at the end as usual. The Lieutenant-Governor made a very charming, welcoming speech, referring amongst other things to my father's great wartime achievements. However, he got quite carried away and ended by asking us all to rise to our feet and drink to the health of 'Lord Montgomery!'

Company at Dinner by Arthur Melville (1858–1904). The importance of postponing, for five or six hours, the principal meal of the day, when hospitality was dispensed and prestigious dishes produced, should not be underestimated. It was accompanied by the development of the habit of 'dressing for dinner', which for men usually involved wearing the newly invented dinner jacket.

ERIC NEWBY

Dinner at the Negresco

The later eating time allowed new foods, new methods of preparation, new ways of serving the various courses, and other social subtleties to indicate the taste, discrimination and financial standing of those partaking. This group, painted in 1872 by Henri Fantin-Latour (1836–1904), is quite clearly an artistic fraternity and one would not enquire too closely about their bank balances.

At Nice we dined at Chantecler, the Negresco's principal restaurant; one of the best restaurants in France; something rare for the restaurant of an *hôtel-palais*. It rates two stars in *Michelin*. Many people think it should have three, but then *Michelin* has never awarded three stars to the restaurant of an *hôtel-palais*. Anyway, it was not *Michelin* that first drew attention to Chantecler. In fact *Michelin* is unable to do so coherently, even if it would like to do so, since it works with symbols rather than words. It was Gault and Millau in their annual survey of French restaurants, *Guide France*. They wrote so extravagantly about the chef, Jacques Maximin, in the 1982 edition, that, reading their advanced and convoluted French, one seriously began to wonder whether they had gone round the culinary bend. They accorded him four chef's *toques* – hats – in red as opposed to black, which indicated that his cooking was *'inventive'* as opposed to *'classique'*, and 19 points out of a possible 20 (which no restaurant has ever received), describing the meal as the *'meilleur repas de l'année'*. This put him in a class with five other immortal chefs, four in France and one in Switzerland, all of whom produced, according to Gault and Millau, *'repas exceptionels de l'année'*.

Maximin came to Chantecler by a circuitous route. At the time we ate his dinner he was thirty-three. At fourteen he began to work in the kitchens of a small hotel, Le Chalet, in his native Le Touquet. Perhaps the most important of his formative years were the two he spent working under Roger Vergé in his restaurant le Moulin de Mougins at Mougins near Cannes, which he himself described as *'la révélation de la cuisine'*.

He came to Chantecler in 1979 from what Gault and Millau described as *'un clinquant* (flashy) *restaurant de Marina-Baie-des-Anges'*, lured there by Madame Augier and her administrator, who carried out the negotiations, agreeing to give him everything he wanted in the way of assistants and the right to cook whatever he chose, buying all the ingredients himself.

That year he was declared Meilleur Ouvrier de France, together with one of his team, Joël Ray, which made them members of a select band of twenty-four which includes Paul Bocuse, the late Jean Troisgros and Alain Chapel. That year, *Michelin* accorded Chantecler its first star and Gault and Millau gave it sixteen points out of twenty. In eighteen months business increased by one hundred per cent.

Not everyone, including the Newbys, goes overboard about the décor at Chantecler. The walls covered with flower-

Au Restaurant Le Doyen *c. 1878, by Ernest Ange Duez (1843–96). In France, as was not the case in Britain at the same time, it was not thought quite so odd for a respectable woman to dine alone. This is a pleasing example of the vogue, current in the 1870s, for 'open air' painting: Degas is said to have remarked of Monet's pictures that they always made him turn the collar of his coat up.*

patterned, genuine seventeenth-century cotton percale, the chairs upholstered in red velvet, the crystal chandeliers are all the product of Madame's discussable taste; but you can't eat the decorations and the table arrangements were beautifully done, and when course after course arrived escorted by the least forbidding sort of *maître d'hotel*, under silver covers that were whipped away simultaneously to reveal dishes of such insubstantial-looking beauty that one was reminded of eighteenth-century water-colours of flowers and vegetables, everything else was forgotten. Among the dishes that we ate were *courgettes â la fleur et aux truffes*, a dish in which the baby vegetables were scooped out, the orange flowers folded and filled with the purée and then cooked in butter with basil, the courgette from which the flower sprouted being sliced, launched into a butter sauce and surmounted with slivers of black truffle. There was also *galette de pigeonneau aux cèpes et girolles*, a fan of underdone slices of pigeon's breast with almonds and a mushroom sauce composed of fresh *cèpes* and *chanterelles*, and, most wonderful of all, *saumon au gros sel et tous les légumes frais*, fresh salmon flown from Scotland, steamed, surrounded by fresh-water crayfish, minute cucumbers, carrots and sliced turnips so small that they could hardly be seen, served with crystals of sea salt, a masterpiece, like no other salmon I have ever eaten. For a sweet we were given one of the creations of Jacques Torres, one of Maximin's adjutants, *gratin de fraises des bois au beurre de Grand Marnier*, wild strawberries in a sort of crême brulée with Grand Marnier. There are two *cartes* for the desserts, one by Torres, the other, with twelve different dishes, by Maximin, all made with chocolate.

This dinner for two, with a bottle of still, red champagne (Pinot France, Laurent Perrier) which cost about 200 francs, produced a bill of £137 ($192) without any liqueurs, twice as much as we had ever spent on a single meal. But in spite of this rudely expensive awakening from what seems in retrospect a beautiful dream, we rose from the table like balloons, thinking about nothing else but where could we lay our hands on a similar amount of money to make possible a return the following day, to eat another version of the best, most imaginative and most beautifully presented meal we have ever eaten in our lives, either on the shores of the Mediterranean or anywhere else.

LORD PALUMBO OF WALBROOK

An Island Idyll

As the fishing boat pulled away from the remote and uninhabited island off the west coast of Scotland, not to return for six days, it evoked in me that mixture of adrenalin and apprehension with which most of us have been familiar at one time or another.

The passengers deposited on the rocky shoreline on that occasion consisted of myself, my German shepherd dog, Jute – now alas the inhabitant of a better world – and an old and valued Argentinian friend with whom I have made many forays to unlikely parts of the world over the years.

Setting up tents can prove to be a difficult manoeuvre if the sea is running and the wind blowing, but with tenacity and

luck we managed the exercise and stowed away our belongings before they became soaked in the all-pervading drizzle. In fading light we struggled across to a rocky outcrop and, crouching beneath it, began deliberately to prepare for dinner, each to his allotted task. Mine – the easier of the two by far – consisted of feeding and watering Jute, preparing the vegetables that we had brought with us, and uncorking the wine! My Argentinian friend revived a boyhood skill on the pampa and busied himself with collecting small pieces of driftwood scattered along the shore, together with a quantity of hemp, string and paper – all from the same source. From such diverse and unpromising beginnings, a fire was soon blazing and a spare tent-pole with a rack of lamb skewered upon it was set into the ground, at an angle to the fire and no more than a metre from it. With a dexterity worthy of the sleight of hand of the most accomplished magician, the angle between pole and fire was constantly increased or diminished until the meat was pronounced well and truly cooked. By this time, the wind and sea had abated – the weather in that part of the world changes more quickly than anywhere else that I have ever encountered – and the sky was bright and clear with stars like diamonds as big as the Ritz. Whether this calm and incomparably beautiful setting, which gave one a very definite sense of one's own presence, distorted everything else by its beneficent glow, I shall never know: but lamb and the red wine that accompanied it have never tasted more delicious; nor, later, have the apfel strudel

'Hip, Hip, Hurrah!' An Artists' Party, Skagen by the Danish painter Peter Severin Kroyer (1851–1909). This is not so much a picnic as a full meal for all the family – of the Scandinavian races, Danes have the reputation of being the jolliest (Hamlet excepted).

Perhaps the Scandinavians made much of summer meals because their winters were so grim and the food available was mostly dried, smoked or salted, like the marinated salmon gravlax, probably invented by the Vikings. To make these offerings attractive, the Danes invented smorrebrod and the Swedes smörgåsbord, the latter accompanied by aquavit. By the late nineteenth century such open sandwiches, originally the evidence of good housewifeliness, had become grand multi-course buffets.

and the sweet white wine chilled to perfection in the sea in an ice bucket of rocks. The memory of it engulfed my sleep that night; invaded my senses in the early morning light, together with the joyful splashing of countless seals taking their first dip of the day; and even now, seven years on, it lingers in the mind's eye as a great and memorable experience.

MICHAEL PARKINSON

Not Cricket

Some dinners remain in the mind because of the people you talk to, rather than the food which is served. I remember nothing at all about the food at the dinner I am going to describe, but I do remember the face of the American lady next to whom I had been seated. Her opening words were: 'They tell me that you know all about cricket, Mr Parkinson. Now I know nothing about the game, have never seen it. Will you kindly explain the rules?'

The soup came and went, then I suppose the fish and the meat, but I remember nothing of it, because I was in full flood describing the mystique of cricket, with my American neighbour nodding her head as the courses went by. We had, I believe, reached the cheese when I finally stopped.

'Well,' said the American lady. 'Well, Michael (may I call you Michael?) that is indeed interesting. Thank you so much. And to think that the teams do all that on *horses*.'

MATTHEW PARRIS

The Dinner that Never Was

Although I normally write about politics, I was recently able to write a book about Peru with hardly a mention of that subject. One incident in the book concerns what I had hoped would be a memorable dinner, eating what the Peruvians had advised us was a memorable dish. This was guinea-pig – *cuy* – and we had to remember to pronounce it *cwee*. It was hard to find, but eventually we were directed to a restaurant where it was a speciality.

The Oven of the Coloured Ladies was a dirty place whose proprietor, head waiter, wine waiter, cook and dishwasher was a Chino-Peruvian who looked like Deng Xiao Ping. Cats peered at us from behind the pillars as we pored over the menu.

There it was! Guinea-pig casserole; seared guinea-pig; guinea-pig with peas and sweet potatoes . . . we had hit the jackpot. Deng Xiao Ping was called.

'One seared *cuy*, please, two *cuy* with peas and. . . .' Deng interrupted.

'No seared *cuy*.'

'Ah. Three *cuy* with peas and. . . .'

'No. No *cuy* with peas and sweet potatoes.'

'Do you have any *cuy* at all?'

'No *cuy* today. Cats eat.'

And we had come so close!

Waiter, There's a Hair in His Soup

In my capacity as Foreign Minister I was accompanying our then Prime Minister, Malcolm Fraser, on a visit to the United States. On arrival in Washington DC we were taken to the Official Guest House, Blair House, accompanied by various Australian and US officials. We proceeded to a formal dinner at Blair House – normally a relaxed affair and hardly memorable.

One Australian official, somewhat sloppy in his habits, sat down for dinner and, complaining of a headache, slipped his hand into his pocket dispensing to himself what he believed were two aspirin. They turned out to be sleeping pills and within ten minutes the official collapsed head first into his soup and slid thereafter under the table, taking with him the meals of both officials on either side of him and disrupting my Prime Minister opposite.

Disaster perhaps, memorable certainly, and, in the process, the disquieting international reputation of some Australians was maintained.

LESTER PIGGOTT

Alas, It Wasn't

Some years ago, there used to be an annual US/UK jockeys' challenge at Sandown Park, which was preceded by a dinner in London, for all those taking part and the organizers and sponsors. It would take place in a private room and generally around a hundred people attended. This particular year, one of the guests brought along Britt Ekland, and she finished up sitting next to me! She turned out to be excellent company, very keen on racing, and was the life and soul of our table of ten. I must admit, her escort kept glaring across the table, and whisked her away as soon as the speeches were over. Throughout the evening a photographer was snapping away at the jockeys and

Through all this conspicuous consumption, the Victorians never forgot the need for charity. Here, the staff are distributing leftovers to the poor after the Lord Mayor's Banquet at the Guildhall in 1882. Servants themselves often had to make do with the remains from their employer's table.

everyone in general, as is the custom at these functions. Months later, in one of the tabloids, a photo appeared of Britt and myself, captioned 'Candlelit Dinner for Two'. Wouldn't that have been a memorable dinner?

LIBBY PURVES

A Formal Dinner

In the summer of 1988, my family set sail on a voyage round the entire coastline of Britain, from the soft, sandy South-East, to the wilder shores of Orkney. I travelled aboard our modern-built gaffer, *Grace O'Malley*, with the children, Nicholas (five) and Rose (three), and my husband Paul. I particularly recall an evening in Wales, when the children were exhausted by their adventures, and fussed horribly at having to row back to our borrowed mooring in the dinghy. Nicholas had developed one of his secret fears about the dinghy ever since the rough row out to the boat at Porth Dinllaen. But as usual, he had his own odd solution to family tension. 'Please may we have a dinner with speeches and proper grown-up behaviour?' he asked. So Paul was toastmaster, banging a wooden spoon; I made a short speech, to the effect that I was honoured to be there; then Nicholas arose with nervous dignity to propose a Vote of Thanks. 'Thank you for the honoured speech, Mrs Heiney, and we hope you like your dinner.' We said Grace, and made adult conversation with each other like, 'Where do you live?' and 'What do you do?' and 'Would you care for some ketchup?' Heaven knows where the idea, or the method, came from: scattered remarks about our public lives, perhaps. But familiarity had probably been breeding a bit too much family contempt; and Nicholas's formal cure for it worked on all our spirits like a charm.

ESTHER RANTZEN

A Bottle-top Tiara

It was a very grand dinner in Mansion House. The invitation was flattering but rather terrifying – a midsummer banquet at which I was to be one of the speakers. I had been lucky enough once before to attend a banquet there and had been entranced by the speakers then, by their wit and eloquence. Could I ever measure up?

My fear was increased by the fact that my agent, who passed the invitation on, added a throwaway postscript, 'Tiaras will be worn.' Oddly enough, there is no Rantzen tiara in the family vaults. I do remember seeing my grandmother in a crown, but it was gold paper, slightly crumpled, and came out of a Christmas cracker. I had the right kind of dress – a beautiful drifting creation of the finest Liberty silk in soft blues and greens, but I simply did not know what to do about the tiara. I rang a friend in the BBC's costume department. Was there anything I could buy, borrow, hire or steal for the night?

He promised to look around for me and, true to his word, the following morning a plastic bag arrived at my desk. I opened it and there inside was an old 'Black and White Minstrels' show-girl's tiara, the sort those lovely ladies with long legs used to wear with satin swimsuits, very high heels, and strange tulle tails. In close-up the tiara was rather tinny and decorated with milk-bottle tops. It needed a piece of elastic to keep it on, but I decided it would do — it would have to do.

The banquet was as glittering and gorgeous as I could possibly have hoped. The men were covered in medals — the women were beautiful in swirling satins, diamonds on their ears and at their throats. Mine was the only tiara. It seemed my agent had not meant it quite as literally as I thought.

My speech was about ChildLine. I had just been answering their phone calls myself and the children's voices were fresh in my head. I have very little memory of my speech, except

Burns Night festivities were a Victorian invention, promoted in large part by expatriate Scots in far-flung corners of the Empire. The celebrations on 25 January, the birthday of the author of 'To A Haggis', now eclipse most other purely Scottish festivals, even St Andrew's Day. The menu for this great feast is usually written in Burns's own Lowland dialect and may include such delicacies as sheep's head broth and wind-dried cod, as well as 'neeps and tatties' (turnips and potatoes) and, of course, whisky. The high spot, shown here, is the piping-in of the haggis which Burns called 'the great chieftain o' the pudden race.' The haggis is then cut by making an incision in its 'paunch' in the shape of St Andrew's cross. The modern recipe for it calls for minced mutton, offal and oatmeal boiled in a sheep's stomach. Burns Night always concludes, as do many other dinners, with the singing of 'Auld Lang Syne', though in fact Burns did not claim this song for his own but said he had overheard it being sung by a shepherd.

It is interesting that Burns, a man so poor that his health was irrevocably ruined from an early age, should have written an ode to haggis, which is a form of 'starvation diet', employing the very last remains of a carcass, the meanest of vegetables, and a cereal which in England was 'a food for horses' (Johnson).

Henry Charles Keith Petty Fitzmaurice, 5th Marquess of Lansdowne, as Viceroy of India, entertains guests beneath a great banyan tree just outside Calcutta in 1893. The boater appears to be as popular as the solar topee, and there are nearly as many servants as there are guests (at least three of whom do not share their companions' very obvious desire to 'watch the birdy'). On the whole, the British empire-builders made little attempt to adapt to local dining customs while abroad, although they adopted a considerable number of 'native' words and expressions, many of which were taken into common usage, among them 'tiffin' (luncheon), 'char' (tea), and 'peg' (alcoholic drink). One of the dishes they did adopt, however, was curry – a name derived from the Tamil word kari, *meaning a relish or sauce for rice. It is said that the British took to the spicy curries because they disguised the poor quality of the meat, which in the Indian heat, and especially before the days of refrigeration, would only keep for a very short time. In truth, however, a good Indian cook would no more use poor meat than would a good European one, although doubtless very bad meals were often disguised with the fiery sauces and concoctions of spices.*

that I tried to express the fear and loneliness of the children who feel they have nowhere else to turn for help except to a counsellor's voice on the 'phone. I described the dedication of the ChildLine team working near St. Paul's, so near this wonderful dinner, bringing comfort and hope to a child's dark, lonely world. I sat down feeling aghast. I had not told a single joke. I felt there was no elegance and style in the speech I had given to that august audience. As I sat down, the knicker elastic around my tinsel tiara snapped and it fell straight into my coffee cup. It was the only laugh I got.

But you never quite know who is in your audience, and how they will respond. We received wonderfully generous donations – whether it was sympathy for my snapped tiara, or whether the voices of those children reached their hearts, I don't know. But it was worth the terror and certainly worth the torn elastic. If any of those kind people read this page, may I thank them from the bottom of my heart on behalf of all ChildLine's children, and apologize for my bottle-top tiara in the coffee cup.

THE HON. SIR DENYS ROBERTS

Another Triumph

I find, from sad experience, that people are only polite when they want something. If they don't, they invariably shout at me. I have been rather hard of hearing since my first wife, who was very excitable before they carried out that frontal lobe surgery on her, threw me down a flight of stairs. This she did solely because, when she suggested that I should get her mother something electrical for her birthday, I had asked her if a chair would do.

So I should have been suspicious of Slimming, when he asked

Amongst the male prerogatives was the right to speak publicly at formal dinners. Here, Lord Salisbury, worried about the Japanese, is telling his audience at the Guildhall Banquet in 1895 that they may 'depend upon it, whatever may happen in that region, be it in the way of war or in the way of commerce, we are equal to any competition which may be proposed to us.' He would not have expressed himself with such confidence on commercial matters had he been speaking one hundred years later.

me, in fulsome tones, if I would speak after dinner to the Commonwealth Press Union.

'It is a very prestigious gathering,' he said.

'Oh,' I replied, to give myself time to think. He had used an impressive word, even if I had not heard it before.

'In fact a lot of other people want to talk to them.'

'In that case you won't need me.'

'We do, dear boy. You are so much better than anybody else.'

That should have warned me, if nothing else did. Nobody calls me dear boy. I don't have that sort of face. If they do, they have preferences which I do not share.

'We only want you to say a few words,' Slimming added persuasively. Unfortunately, this phrase does not mean what it says, rather like 'Yes, darling, we'll wait until after we're married.' What the host expects is a full-scale speech, which will compensate for dreadful food, for the vinegar-like wine and for the high level of personal hostility which infects those who have assembled with a common purpose. Mind you, if he really meant what he said, the insult would have been unpardonable.

I arrived at the Miramar Hotel at eight o'clock, as Slimming had asked. The place was full of people looking lost, whom I assumed to be delegates to the conference. The sad women were probably their wives, the cheerful ones their mistresses. There was nobody to meet me, as Slimming had promised. I followed the others, who seemed to be making their way towards

A Thanksgiving Day dinner in the 1850s – although if the host is carving the traditional turkeys, they are quite exceptionally miserable birds. A religious and social festival in the United States, Thanksgiving is (generally) held on the last Thursday in November. The custom originated with the first settlers on the east coast of America (where wild turkeys were plentiful), the Pilgrims setting aside a special day for thanksgiving after their first successful harvest in 1621 – it did not become a fully national custom until President Lincoln's proclamation in 1864. The Thanksgiving turkey is invariably served with cranberry sauce, as this fruit, too, was found in abundance near the early settlements.

Turkeys were brought to western attention by the Spanish explorers of Mexico, who found them, already domesticated by the Mexicans, on their first expedition of 1518; a northern strain of the bird was also discovered in the eastern areas settled by Europeans, and they first seem to have arrived in Europe in the early sixteenth century. The name is confusing, and its origin uncertain – early settlers confused the turkey with the guinea fowl, which was also known as a 'turkey fowl', either because it was exported to Europe through Turkey, or because of identification with the Asian strain of that bird, at a time when Muhammadans were often referred to generically as 'Turks'. Another theory is that the name derives from the bird's call, 'turk-turk-turk'. Certainly English is the only European language to use the name 'turkey' or any of its derivatives.

a large room. Outside it was a notice reading 'Welcome to the Delegates to the Annual Meeting of Acupuncturists.'

I knew that acupuncture works, as I have yet to see a sick porcupine, but I hoped it was not the right conference. Mind you, I would put nothing beyond Slimming, who would do anything to get a speaker.

As I hesitated, he saw me, waving with the ivory cigarette holder which he used in the belief that it would prevent him getting lung cancer.

'I've been looking for you everywhere,' he said accusingly. 'You are in the wrong place.'

'Everyone has to be somewhere, you know,' I answered, deciding that subtler arguments would be wasted on him.

'It doesn't make my job any easier when you hide,' he grumbled. 'I expect you lost your nerve.'

'Yes,' I admitted. 'That is why I joined the needle men.'

'Look here, old man, do you mind keeping it short and very amusing?'

'You said I should talk for a quarter of an hour.'

'That is the usual length, but they would like you to be a bit shorter, before the dancing, and after the Chiu Chow opera.

There are several kinds of Chinese opera, all of them tuneless to Western ears, though some acquire a degree of attractiveness after the first five hours. But not Chiu Chow opera. During the disturbances in Hong Kong, political slogans, interspersed with allegations about the sexual preferences and parentage of prominent local people, were being broadcast from the Bank of China. Chiu Chow opera was beamed back by the police from loudspeakers set up round the Bank. Even the diehard left-wingers had had enough after three hours and switched off their loudspeakers.

'The Chiu Chow opera will be finished during dinner,' he went on. 'Then we'll give them five minutes to ease themselves.'

'We mustn't miss that,' I agreed.

'Then I tell them that you would like to speak for about five

THANKSGIVING DAY—THE DINNER.

minutes and that you are going to amuse them.'

'I'd rather you didn't say that, as I don't suppose I will.'

Dinner began punctually at eight. Many of the guests was already full of alcohol and were laughing at anything. The Chiu Chow opera soon fixed that. There is nothing amusing about that noise. The opera continued well beyond dinner and had the effect of stifling all conversation, not that this seemed to matter much as I was on the end of a long table, with only one neighbour, a blonde girl of uncertain age who was emerging from the top of her dress. She was so covered in pimples that she was generally known as 'the acne carriage'. During the opera, her ears were packed with bread, which protected her against it and any conversation with myself. As the opera continued, the audience began to fall asleep, its humour steadily deteriorating. It was close to eleven o'clock when Slimming clapped me on the shoulder, with simulated pleasure, and told me that I would be speaking soon.

'The band is waiting,' he added. 'Try not to be too long, there's a good chap. About four minutes will do. I will take you on stage as soon as the opera stops and announce you myself.'

'I shall be quite happy not to say anything at all, Slimming.'

'They're expecting it, your name is on the menu.' It was, in small letters on the left, underneath the menu and opposite to 'poisson' misspelt with one 's'.

The opera ended, with a final wail from the singers and a last uncoordinated salvo from the drums. It was close to eleven o'clock. Slimming led me to the stage, as the applause died

The Restaurant *by F. S. Zhuravlov. Russians have a reputation for taking drink more seriously than food. Towards the end of the eighteenth century it was estimated that the male inhabitants of St Petersburg were consuming ninety pints of spirits per head per annum. These nineteenth-century Russians, however, certainly seem to making up in quantity for whatever their meal may lack in quality. Russia is a major source of supply for one of the most prized delicacies at any dinner, baluga and sturgeon caviare.*

away. It had been genuine, as nobody had believed that the opera would ever end and they wished to show their appreciation of their deliverance.

'I should think three minutes will do,' he muttered at me. 'Just time for the band to tune up.'

He introduced me as the representative of the Government, who would say a few words and welcome the delegates, and asked everyone to be back in their seats in five minutes as the band would then play for dancing. I made the mistake of looking around me as I spoke. I have learned not to do this, but to look at my notes, in the shifty way which reminds many of the audience of the last time they bought a second-hand car.

Behind me were the trappings of the opera, none of which seemed to have much reference to it, or to my speech, even the truncated version. When I began, there were crimson floating panels, a backdrop showing a badly dredged lake, a wooden bed and a heap of cymbals. What I did not then know was that the stage hands were removing them.

I thought that the interest which I saw in the audience must be due to something I had said. I did not realize that it was more interested in whether or not the stage hand, who was trying to carry too much, would drop the furniture. He did, to some applause, which occurred in the middle of one of my sentences.

In front of me was a microphone, which was not working, and an audience which was sparse. Most of them had left the hall to relieve themselves, before the dancing, which was the only reason why many of them had come. They drifted back, talking noisily among themselves.

I do not recall what I said, except that I know it was witty, informative and wise, or at least my fifteen-minute speech would have been if I had delivered it. After I had been speaking for about three minutes, through a torrent of noise from the audience, the stage began to turn. Slimming had omitted to warn me that there was a revolving stage. Nor, in view of the fact that two of them fell over, did anyone seem to have told the scene shifters. This caused the loudest laugh of the evening.

As I disappeared, still talking bravely, the dance band came into view, to be greeted by loud cheers. I found myself backstage, alone, except for the dead microphone. I sadly put my notes in my pocket and waited for someone to rescue me, sitting on a Chiu Chow drum which seemed also to have been abandoned.

A few minutes later, Slimming bounded in, full of enthusiasm.

'Well done, old man,' he shouted. 'Just the ticket. The perfect aperitif.' I did not remind him that even the Chinese, with their preference for doing things back to front, did not take an aperitif after dinner.

'Did you hear the audience applauding as you revolved? What you said was much appreciated.'

'What did I say?' I asked.

'That has nothing to do with it. I must dash off and see to the President of the Press Union. He has just fallen downstairs.'

'I hope it was from laughing at my speech.'

'Heavens no. It was a real accident.'

Slimming led me back to my table, where the blonde girl was sitting alone. Everyone else had gone.

'Hello,' she asked, 'Where have you been?'

'Actually, I've been making a speech.'

'Oh, was that you up there?' I nodded. 'I couldn't hear a word. Was it good?'

'I suppose it was. At least, there was a good round of applause when I finished.' I thought I had better salvage what I could.

'Was that for you? Surely it was for the band?'

JANCIS ROBINSON

Gourmandise at Yquem

In July 1986 I received a very puzzling invitation. The time and place were clear enough. I was bid for 11 a.m. on 30 September to Château d'Yquem, indisputably the greatest property in Sauternes, the sweet wine district south-east of Bordeaux. The host was quite plain too: Herr Hardy Rodenstock, perhaps the most famous of a new group of near-fanatical fine wine collectors in Germany. But *what* exactly was I being invited to?

In the English part of the trilingual invitation, it was described simply as a 'wine tasting with rare wines' which 'will end at about 10 p.m.' I was told to wear a metaphorical black tie, that my invitation was for one person only and was not transferable, and that I should reply, by registered post, by 30 August. I reckoned that any event to which a typical German postman should not be relied upon to convey my acceptance would probably be worth going to. I was right.

The 'wine tasting with rare wines' turned out to be a twelve-course meal to which forty of us sat down at about noon on

Dining together at a 'common board' had been a feature of monastic life and is still continued by the students of the ancient universities. Here female undergraduates are saying grace before dinner at Girton College, Cambridge, founded in 1869, one of the first to educate women. Note the institutional sparseness and austerity of the scene, in spite of the pot-plants on the table, which contrasts markedly with the rituals and convivial atmosphere of the older colleges.

These undergraduates in the Hall at Trinity, Cambridge, by comparison, are dining in splendid surroundings, under the gaze of many illustrious alumni of their college. They are being waited on by the college servants (or gyps), while the dons sit at the high table beneath the royal arms. Nowadays many Oxbridge colleges have gone self-service and have excused the wearing of gowns, except on special occasions.

Tuesday and from which we got up at one o'clock on Wednesday morning. We were each served *sixty-six* different wines, not to taste – that would have been easy – but to *drink*. There was not a spittoon in sight, until about eight o'clock in the evening when Michael Broadbent (under whose hammer a good proportion of all that we enjoyed must have passed a time or two), finally secured a rather grand-looking *cache-pot* for himself and his neighbours. Around 3500 splinter-stemmed crystal glasses were, in sobering progression, cleaned, filled, emptied, and cleaned again. Thank heavens I stopped myself, at the last minute, wearing a new skin-tight frock. The seams would never have withstood the strain. As luck would have it, I wore indulgently elastic black on that exquisite autumn morning. There was more that a hint of Glyndebourne as we foregathered on the lawns in front of the château, our shamelessly sophisticated clothing somehow at odds with the natural beauty of the setting.

Château d'Yquem is in a commanding position, both literally and figuratively, in this almost archaically rural corner of France. The fortified *château-fermier* stands on Sauternes' only hilltop and from under its spreading cedars we could see row upon row of world-famous vines stretching through the crisp sunshine into the smoky blue distance, patiently awaiting the development of the 'noble rot' that makes great sweet wines even greater and sweeter by attacking them, concentrating the sugar and flavour elements. This was the crucial time of year for the umpteenth-generation guardian of Château d'Yquem, Comte Alexandre de Lur-Saluces, who was waiting to see whether, now that he had a vineyard full of ripe, healthy grapes, the succeeding mists of autumn would favour the spread of this magical fungus. (It did.)

At this stage the two chefs needed to fuel us through the forthcoming marathon, Rolf-Dieter Jung of the Restaurant Fuente in Mülheim and Francis Garcia of Bordeaux's Restaurent Clavel, came out into the sunshine to give us, literally, a taste of what was to come (their whites already smelt of complex reductions). They'd arrived at 5 a.m. and couldn't stop themselves saying *bonsoir*. Since the château is uninhabited (the Lur-Saluces live in Bordeaux), the poor old kitchen must have suffered the shock of its life that day.

We filed into the château past an easel on to which a copy of the poster-sized menu had been pinned. Those of us who examined it had the curious sensation of feeling our stomachs churn as our palates salivated. Surely they couldn't mean to give us every one of those 16 vintages of Ygrec, the mind-blowingly alcoholic dry wine of Yquem? And a blind tasting of ten clarets from vintages 1937 back to 1848? Such an exercise might mean something to the likes of Hardy and his fellow Feinschmeckers, whose cellars are lined with pre-phylloxera bottles, but those of us with more limited experience of these vintages would be delighted by the unadorned chance to savour any one of these clarets in isolation. Were we really to be served *homard*, *langoustines*, *foie gras*, *cèpes* and *truffes* at the same meal? And what about the Yquem listed as '*c. 1750*'?

See the naughty restless child
Growing still more rude and wild,
Till his chair falls over quite.
Philip screams with all his might,
Catches at the cloth, but then
That makes matters worse again.
Down upon the ground they fall,
Glasses, plates, knives, forks and all.
How Mamma did fret and frown,
When she saw them tumbling down!
And Papa made such a face!
Philip is in sad disgrace.

As we took our places in the light, sunny dining-room over-looking the vineyards on one side and the nicely rustic courtyard on the other, we were each presented with a splendid red-velvet-bound tasting album (whose dimensions were such as to hamper severely the quite stunning *service* over the next thirteen hours). I felt very grand at being put, in this the first of three varied *placements*, next to the Count and opposite Hardy.

The Count told me without rancour that Hardy, who is known as Herr Yquem in Germany, had tasted far more vintages of Yquem than he, the owner, had. 'He probably still owns more than me too,' he added. Then he opened his album and, looking at the title page, asked Hardy what the figure seven on it meant. 'It means its the seventh such rare wine tasting that I have organized,' explained Hardy simply. The Count nodded glumly. 'That's what I thought it meant,' he said in a subdued sort of way.

Hardy Rodenstock could hardly be a less ostentatious character. He throws not a kilo of his modest weight about; he is merely absolutely fascinated by wine and appears to devote to it every waking minute left to him by his obviously flourishing career in the music business. It was Hardy, for instance, who acquired the much-publicized bottles of wine from the 1780s, supposedly ordered by Thomas Jefferson. He must have spent weeks organizing this extravaganza which, even the Count admitted, was not a special tasting, but a world first.

Hardy had even conducted blind water tastings to ensure that his priceless bottles were rinsed down with H_2O in its most harmonious form. (Spa waters, still and sparkling, were chosen; I must have got through several litres.)

Well, we couldn't put it off any longer. We had to get going on this marathon consumption. A flight of four German wines was served first, including a Beerenauslese Trocken, if you please (a 'sweet dry' curiosity since banned by the German authorities), with a 'simple' salad of red mullet, artichokes and potatoes.

The *cassolette de homard aux perles de légumes* was temptingly rich for the second of a dozen courses, but the four white burgundies served with it were utterly distracting – particularly a rivetingly pure brace of Bienvenue Bâtard-Montrachets, 1979 and 1982, from André Ramonet.

Our sixteen Ygrecs followed with two more fish courses and suggested conclusively to me that this dry wine does not improve with more than ten years in bottle, but they served admirably to heighten the high point of this day-long succession of high points, a run of five vintages of Château d'Yquem, the sweet wine and no messing, that marked the end of our first session at the table. Before our sliver of fresh *foie gras* sautéed with white grapes and Yquem 1976 (it's no good describing wines as '76 in a Hardy context), we were to taste Yquem 1858, 1847, 1811 and one amazing bottle that had been put at about 1750.

Hardy, who has never disclosed exactly how or where in Paris he unearthed the Thomas Jefferson bottles, had heard that there were still some treasures from the former Tsars' cellars to be found in Leningrad. Yquem had long been a favourite with the Russian court, the Tsar having paid 20,000 gold francs for a barrel of Yquem in 1847 in one well-documented transaction. He managed to find this bottle, flask-shaped and deep indigo-coloured glass engraved all over with tiny white painted flowers

grapes and vine leaves, as was the custom then, and marked with the arms of the Sauvage family (who did not transfer ownership of Yquem by marriage into the Lur-Saluces family till 1785).

Analysis of the glass, once Hardy had somehow spirited the bottle out of the USSR, suggested that it was mid-eighteenth century, making this wine that we were about to taste the oldest that had probably ever been tasted from a bottle. (Great sweet white wines probably stand a better chance of survival over a few hundred years than most, and several of those present had drooled over a Thomas Jefferson bottle of Yquem 1784 at the previous year's event in Germany.)

But first we had to eat our bread and butter – and what bread and butter! The nineteenth-century Yquems, culled from cellars as far apart as Scotland and Venezuela, had turned deep tawny as very old white wines are wont to do, but tasted by no means over the hill. The 1858 was starting to be a little aggressive and the 1811 was perhaps a bit attenuated, but the 1874 was absolutely great wine, utterly alive and kicking, very vigorous, round and rich with good acid balance and a lovely long, well-integrated flavour that just went on and on.

Silence fell as the young sommelier imported from Munich tapped away at the most ancient bottle of all. Then came a communal squeal of delight as the cork emerged intact, only to crumble immediately, exhausted by the effort of preserving this wine so long. There was just one bottle, which everyone wanted to touch, enough for a good-sized glass for each of the four tables. When it was poured, it looked almost like claret, so deep-coloured and red was it. The temptation was to admire and

The Artist's dinner party, 1903. *There is something particularly engaging about Scandinavian depictions of dinners – as with this painting of Viggo Johansen's own dinner-party. Perhaps the terrible winters, particularly in the far north where famine was often close behind, helped to create a special tradition of celebratory dinners in the spring or summer. Such a dinner became the subject of a full-length feature film,* Babette's Feast, *the first time that a dinner was celebrated in the cinema.*

comment, but Michael Broadbent, with the natural sense of slightly bossy responsibility that has got him where he is, reminded us sharply that this was very old wine that should be tasted immediately, before it faded.

There is no way four glasses, however beautiful (they were specially made and engraved for this particular wine by Riedel), can be shared elegantly by forty tasters, but somehow everyone managed to taste this extraordinary liquid: deep foxy red, creamy rich in texture, almost unctuous with a slight minerally edge, just starting to fall apart, but still very definitely a top quality, naturally sweet wine. What an experience, to think that we were tasting a wine made perhaps twenty years before Napoleon was even born.

The special glasses were duly auctioned for charity, the Count nobly setting a price of 12,000 francs for the first set of four. I felt sorry for Michael Broadbent who, after tasting thirty-odd wines, and making one of his extra-thorough notes on each, was expected to conduct the sale.

By now it was five in the afternoon and the golden autumn light was gently fading. We were all dying to get outside before it disappeared so, pausing only to savour the *foie gras* and 1976 Yquem, we trooped outside, the earnest ones for a tour of the cellars, the Brits for a quiet nap under the tree.

Now, I think you probably have some idea of how the rest of the day went by now. Yes, there was more of the same, only a little bit different. 'Standout' wines among the thirty-three that followed included Château Canon 1966 from a jeroboam and Calon-Ségur 1966 from an imperial (the equivalent of six and eight bottles respectively in one); Château Pétrus and Cheval Blanc in magnum, both 1921; a jeroboam of Château Mouton-Rothschild 1929 that, even at ten o'clock with Brillat-Savarin and *pain noir aux pruneaux*, was so sensationally complete it revived my flagging spirits; and two more absolutely gorgeous vintages of Château d'Yquem, 1937 and 1921.

The staff of the château and restaurants had behaved beautifully, with admirable manners and stamina throughout, but how about the guests? Since that day, a lot of people have asked me, some more politely than others, but weren't you all horribly *drunk*? And the answer, amazingly enough, is no. Funnily enough, for me and I suspect many others, the day turned into almost a battle for survival rather than an opportunity to maximize consumption. Although I consciously sipped rather than drank, I did find myself flushing down an Anadin with some Lanson 1964 at about eight o'clock (a practice which I'm sure should not be condoned on any basis). Next morning I felt eerily healthy, even when I got up at 6 a.m. to catch the red-eye special back to Heathrow. I did notice the in-flight breakfast wasn't up to much though.

ANITA RODDICK

The Biter Un-bit

Travel is a tonic for me. I find it cures whatever's ailing me. But there have been moments when remedy comes danger- ously close to inducing malady. One such moment brought about a memorable dinner in Mexico City.

I had been taken to a restaurant called Meson de Alonso where I was promised real Mayan cooking, at that time a culinary craze among Mexicans rediscovering their history. Someone neglected to tell me that a primary pre-Columbian protein source was

THE STORY OF AUGUSTUS WHO WOULD NOT HAVE ANY SOUP.

Augustus was a chubby lad;
Fat ruddy cheeks Augustus had;
And every body saw with joy
The plump and hearty healthy boy.
He ate and drank as he was told,
And never let his soup get cold.
But one day, one cold winter's day,
He scream'd out — "Take the soup away!
O take the nasty soup away!
I won't have any soup to-day."

Next day, now look, the picture shows
How lank and lean Augustus grows!
Yet, though he feels so weak and ill,
The naughty fellow cries out still —
"Not any soup for me, I say:
O take the nasty soup away!
I won't have any soup to-day."

The third-day comes; Oh what a sin!
To make himself so pale and thin.
Yet, when the soup is put on table,
He screams, as loud as he is able, —
"Not any soup for me, I say:
O take the nasty soup away!
I won't have any soup to-day."

Look at him, now the fourth day's come!
He scarcely weighs a sugar-plum;
He's like a little bit of thread,
And on the fifth day, he was — dead!

actually insects. The first clue was the dish of bar-snacks – deep-fried grasshoppers. Then the chef, whose reputation ranges all the way to Dallas, proudly presented a cavalcade of bugs that the deep fryer hadn't managed to transform into anything more edible. Speciality of the house was a taco filled with live beetles that scurried off the cheeks of the diner unless you were quick enough to poke them back into your mouth. I saw none of this because I kept my menu clapped over my face until the bill was settled and we could leave. So my most memorable meal came to a close without a bite of food passing my lips. Call me craven, but I'm not ready to bite into anything that's liable to bite back.

JEAN ROOK

A Lost Bet

This dinner is burned on my mind like a pan of boiling fat. I was asked to address the expensive annual dinner of a stag group (to describe them as an all-male organization would be a euphemism) at the Savoy Hotel. The Yuppies concerned were in advertising or double-glazing. I can't remember which, but they were a typical Yuppie herd of very pushy twenty-plus-year-olds with very clean finger nails, very short haircuts, and very loud, domineering voices.

During flowing pre-dinner drinks, the most obnoxious of these whizz-bang kids informed me that they'd never had a woman speaker before, they took bets on how long speeches would last (his bet on me was 29 minutes) and 'if we find speakers boring, we put our feet up on the tables and go to sleep.'

I asked my old chum, toastmaster Ivor Spencer, to make a note of the man's face, and his table, and to tip me off where he was seated.

As I rose to face the silently sneering mob who had paid me a hell of whack for the pleasure of expressing their wonder that a mere fool of a woman earned three times as much as they did, Ivor nudged me, 'the bloke you want is on Table 10.'

My opening speech ran: 'Mr President and the man on Table 10 who has made a bet that I shall speak for 29 minutes. I have borrowed a stop watch (I had, too) to ensure that I shall speak for 28½ or 29½ minutes, so Table 10 has just lost a tenner.

I am further informed by you, sir, on Table 10 that, if you get bored with my speech, you will put your feet up on the table and go to sleep. Having met you, I can give you one assurance . . . you will never, never sleep with me.'

I have to say the young lions listened like shorn lambs and, the split second I wrapped up, at 31¼ minutes, the chap on Table 10 bolted, like a stag, into the night.

MICHAEL ROUX

Indulge or Refrain

Every year on 26 December, The Waterside Inn closes its doors for a good six weeks and my wife and I crawl onto a jet plane and head towards a destination which will soothe the aching body and scattered brain. The first few days are mute, so there is always the search for the pleasure of the palate to cover those silences over dinner.

In 1988, Robyn and I set out for Sydney on a direct flight. Normally we break the flight, but for her family reasons we had to be there straight away. We always go straight to Palm Beach, about 45 minutes from Sydney. I love it there. The air is sweet, the breeze gentle and, because most of our friends have already been summering themselves in lethargy for some weeks, they are soothing and kind. Before leaving Bray, I telephoned a friend called Michael McMahon, who at the time owned a restaurant called Barrenjoey House in Palm Beach. 'Michael,' I said, 'nous sommes en route, command les Mud Crabs, the rest of the menu is up to you.' Michael's reply is unprintable, but in good Aussie fashion, he replied 'She'll be right.'

We arrived bruised, tired, jetlagged and generally in a condition of 'too far gone . . . terminal!' Our friend, seeing our condition, thought it prudent to keep his distance. As we settled into our canvas chairs under the palm trees, a glass of chilled white was poured and the vocal cords muttered 'delicious, give me more.' We were drinking a Petaluma Rhine Reisling, from South Australia, which was fruity, crisp and a delicious hit to the palate. Then arrived an enormous white porcelain bowl groaning with Mud Crab, with the steam rising and the aroma pervading the warm air. I broke one of the claws and decided that should

In nineteenth-century London, there was a dearth of good places to dine. Only a few high-class chop-houses had the reputation enjoyed by Simpson's in the Strand and by 1850 visitors to the Great Exhibition found it difficult to discover first-class restaurants, except for a handful of French establishments. There were few hotels of eminence in the West End, and the Savoy, bought by Richard D'Oyly Carte, of opera fame, did not open its restaurant until 1889. It was managed by César Ritz who brought the brilliant chef Auguste Escoffier to its kitchens. There are no women dining at the Savoy in this illustration, but Ritz soon began private dining-rooms for such famous hostesses as Lady Randolph Churchill and Consuela Vanderbilt, Duchess of Marlborough.

my call from the almighty be at that second, he would have to wait until I had finished the bowl. The flesh was so sweet, moist and rich; the meat falls in chunks, satisfying the palate and yet driving one crazy for another mouthful. Our hands, our faces, our glasses were covered with our greedy pleasure.

Another porcelain bowl appeared with lemon, hot water and white towels for bathing. We had now managed to string a few words together which almost resembled a sentence. A small plate of crab meat was placed in front of us. With the work done for us and the effect of the Reisling, I truly thought I was in fact going to survive the day. The crab meat had been lightly marinated in lime juice, and garnished with sun-dried tomatoes. Another South Australian wine in the shape of a bottle of Mount Adam Chardonnay arrived. . . . What is next, I thought, fish? No, it was yet more Mud Crab sautéed with a touch of lemon grass, a hint of chilli and soya sauce. The depth of this Chardonnay, which I believe to be the best in Australia, was a perfect foil for the aromatics of this dish.

To that evening and since I have never been able to eat the same product, three times in one meal. It is against everything I believe in terms of a balance of ingredients. The challenge was still out of course because there was dessert to come. Michael finally left the white flag flying and came to join us. I am not a man known to lose his words, especially after a stunning meal. I was so soporific by this time, I could barely stop the tears of a man returned from the dead.

To complete this wonderful over-indulgence of Mud Crab, we finished with a perfect white peach which was so sweet in its natural state, I felt the only compliment to it was to pour a little of the 1979 Bollinger R.D., which Michael had so thoughtfully arrived with, to celebrate the return of the power of speech.

As the nineteenth century gave way to the twentieth, it became more common for British men and women – of the higher and more moneyed classes – to dine together in public. Albert Chevallier Tayler's An Elegant Soirée *perhaps shows people dining after the theatre; they appear to be in a restaurant, rather than a private house.*

It was then I listened to the challenge I had laid for him. As we normally arrive in Australia somewhat later in January, I, like a spoilt tourist, thought the Mud Crabs were available all summer. Apparently Michael bribed every supplier and restaurateur from one end of the east coast to another in search of Mud Crabs. Collected in the early hours that morning, I understand we ate our way through the entire supply. I have no conscience. It merely confirms my belief that no delicacy should be taken in small quantities. Indulge or Refrain. With a minor slip-up in the country of origin of the champagne, these were Australian ingredients at their best, prepared to perfection and beyond competition.

NED SHERRIN

Second Helpings

When I was Messing Officer in the Royal Corps of Signals Mess in Beethoven Strasse, Klagerfurt, Austria, I arranged a dinner so awful that my fellow officers swore that they could all immediately eat another dinner at the Landhaus Keller in town. I took on the bet and took them out – having foolishly already taken my precautionary Alka Seltzers. I then, like them, downed an enormous mixed grill – chops, steaks, eggs, sausages, and drank a lot more. I was ill for several days and have never forgotten or tried to emulate it.

The Visit of the German Emperor to Cowes: The Banquet to His Majesty on Board the Royal Yacht Victoria and Albert. *Kaiser Wilhelm II, one of the many grandchildren of Queen Victoria, succeeded his father as Emperor of Germany and King of Prussia in 1888. The then Prince of Wales, later King Edward VII, was a keen sailor, and his interest and patronage helped to make both the sport and Cowes popular and fashionable. Victoria and Albert was not much like the general idea of a yacht, all sails and America's Cup; a substantial iron ship, powered by steam, she was held on the Navy's strength and commanded by an admiral. Today's Royal Yacht, HMS Britannia, on which many royal dinners now take place, is designed to be used as a hospital ship in the event of war.*

RICHARD SHEPHERD

The Vice of the Lobster

A very good friend of mine, who is, incidentally, my doctor, invited me to dinner at his house in Marylebone. He said that he was having live Maine lobsters flown in that day: they were being collected from the airport at half past six that evening and dinner would be at nine o'clock. (I should explain that the reason he was having American lobsters flown in was to surprise his wife, who is an American.) I told him that I was working that evening, but would try to get off around ten o'clock, but that he shouldn't worry about feeding me. I should also add that he did not tell me who the rest of the guests were.

On leaving the restaurant that night, I put on a brand new suit, a fairly expensive one at that, thinking that I would be polite, go over, pay my respects, have a drink and then toodle off down to Tramp to have some supper. On arriving at his house, I was completely taken aback, as all the guests were friends of mine from fifteen years back. My doctor's wife insisted that I sit down and eat, as they had kept a lobster for me. I said that really I was fine and she shouldn't bother, but everyone insisted that I sit down and join the party.

The lobster was duly placed in front of me and the lady of the house went to fetch the melted butter. Within seconds she returned with a saucepan containing approximately one kilo of hot, molten butter and deposited the whole lot in my lap. There was a stunned silence, broken only by the hostess as she dashed from the room, apologizing profusely. The lobster, I might add, was delicious, but the incident certainly curtailed any plans I might have had earlier.

Butter isn't the most comfortable food to wear whilst eating, but by the time I got to the second bottle of wine, I was no longer feeling any pain!

LADY SOAMES

Dinner at Chartwell

Meal-times were the highlights of the day at Chartwell, both from the point of view of food and entertainment. The 'basic' house-party, enlarged by other guests, usually formed a gathering it would be hard to beat for value. There was little warming up; the conversation plunged straight into some burning or vital question. But the talk was by no means confined to politics; it ranged over history, art, and literature; it toyed with philosophical themes; it visited the past and explored the future. 'The Prof' [Lindemann] and his slide-rule were much in demand on all scientific problems. Sometimes the conversation was a ding-dong battle of wits and words between, say, Winston and Duff Cooper, with the rest of the company skirmishing on the sidelines and keeping the score. The verbal pyrotechnics waxed hot and fierce, usually dissolving in an instant into gales of laughter. General conversation usually dwindled, as nearly everyone wanted to share the main 'entertainment', whether it was a discussion, or a dramatic or compelling monologue from Winston. Perhaps most enjoyable of all, particularly to us children (who from an early age partook of dining-room life)

The writer of London at Table, *a sort of* Good Food Guide *of the 1850s, had complained that 'one evil of long standing still exists in London, and that is the difficulty of finding an Hotel or Restaurant where strangers of the fair sex may be taken to dine.' By comparison, Josef Engelhart's painting* Dinner With Friends *(1903) catches the glitter of Viennese café society in the years before the Great War destroyed the last remnants of the Austro-Hungarian Empire.*

were the days when the Muse of Poetry and of Song held sway: when from the incredible store of our father's memory would flow verse sacred and profane, heroic and frivolous, in glorious profusion. Many a time a luncheon party broke up only after the completion of a near word-perfect recitation of 'Horatius'. (Very popular with the children, as we could join in 'the brave days of old' bits.)

If 'high thinking' could be said to be a feature of life at Chartwell, it did not go hand-in-hand with 'plain living'; the hospitality was lavish and the food delicious. Clementine rarely had a highly-trained cook, she could not afford one; more often than not she had a talented kitchen-maid, whom she would 'develop' herself. This was long before the period when cook-hostesses became a commonplace, but Clementine knew a great deal about delicious food and the theory of cooking, and she was highly successful in imparting her knowledge, never grudging time or trouble spent on planning and disussing the food with her cook. Naturally, what with the food and the talk, meal-times tended to prolong themselves far into the afternoon or evening. It was unusual at a weekend to leave the dining-room after luncheon before half past three or even four o'clock, and in the evenings the men stayed on endlessly after the women had gone to the drawing-room. Clementine found this habit increasingly trying as the years went by, and on one or two occasions marked her displeasure by taking the women off to bed, leaving a deserted drawing-room to greet the men when they eventually appeared, headed by Winston, full of guilty apologies.

Clementine rarely tried to compete against Winston in conversation during these long, verbose meals. However riveting the topics, she was always alert and attentive to the food and the service. She was, fortunately, a good listener, and for the most part enjoyed the arguments. But she sometimes tired of the monologues and would firmly try, with varying degrees of success, to resurrect some form of general conversation. She could herself be a sparkling talker, with a sense of wit, and she laughed uproariously at times. In argument she often waxed passionate and partisan, and when the talk took a tone or direction of which she disapproved, she would after a time suddenly 'erupt', and could maul most savagely those of whose views or character she either temporarily or habitually disapproved. The fact that they were her guests at the time afforded them no protection. Very occasionally, having delivered herself of her opinion, she simply rose and swept out, leaving her children puce with embarrassment, and any women guests flustered and uncertain as to whether they should 'sweep' too.

When Clementine was really roused, even Winston could not restrain her; and although these violent outbursts embarrassed him at the time, he would often recount the incident afterwards with a sort of rueful pride: 'Clemmie gave poor —— a most fearful mauling.'

JACKIE STEWART

Bowing Out

A dinner I will never forget was the one given by the Ford Motor Company at the Savoy Hotel at the end of 1973 to commemorate my retirement from motor racing.

Ford had very generously suggested that I ask as many of my friends as possible to attend. On that occasion I was able to bring together many of my past team-mates, team managers, team owners, school friends, and more recent friends. Almost everyone who was there had played some part in my professional life as a driver, or in my earlier shooting days.

Ford, in their usual professional fashion, had collected all sorts of photographs which they had enlarged and displayed on the walls of the room used for pre-dinner cocktails.

When I walked into the already-assembled group in the dining-room, everyone was sporting Jackie Stewart caps and sun-glasses which had been distributed beforehand. What a sight it was!

The meal was extremely nice, but the speeches were what it was all about. On that evening – 19 December 1973 – a William McGonagall reading was performed by the late John Lawrie. Walter Hayes, then Vice President, Public Affairs, Ford, Stuart Turner, their Director of Motor Sport, and Ken Tyrrell, my great Team Manager, all spoke, with varying degrees of abuse, about my time behind the wheel. And, of course, I was allowed to respond!

Ken Tyrrell presented me with Chassis No. 003 Tyrrell Ford, the car that had helped me win the World Championship in 1971 and some other Grands Prix in 1972. For me it was an evening never to be forgotten, surrounded by so many of the people who had contributed to my success and supported me for all those years in one form or another – a wonderful dinner!

SERENA SUTCLIFFE

Memories of Twenty Years Ago

As I write this, events in Lithuania cause me to remember, more vividly than I would have wished, another crushing erosion of liberty for those who live under Soviet rule. My mind goes back to the dinner I shared in Moscow on the night of 20/21 August 1968, accompanied by the knowledge that Soviet troops were swarming all over Prague.

My sorrow was that of a spectator, but the Russian who ate with me then was numb with more personal grief and the defeat of hope. He had thought that the Prague Spring was the opening of a door. He had, I knew, struggled with increasing difficulty to justify the system under which he had been brought up, and the supposed thaw was the last floating piece of debris to cling to. It went that night, and he cried. I had never before seen a beautiful, brilliant, young man cry. He was, I am sure, already being watched, for he had been tainted with uncanny linguistic ability and contact with Scandinavia and Britain. I do not know where he is now. We drank koskenkorva that I had brought from Finland and ate caviar from a tin. The room was small and cramped. We listened to *Ein Heldenleben*. It was scratched and grainy, not like the transcendental Tilson Thomas sound I heard later, in a cruel twist, as the Soviet 'security forces' (what a term of mockery) were beating young boys in Vilnius.

I felt as impotent now to comfort or to help as I had over twenty years ago in Moscow.

The imagination should not dwell too much on what it must be like to dine on the restricted menu available to besieged citizens — like those of the Commune of Paris in 1871, who were surrounded not only by a victorious German army but also by their own soldiers, the latter trying to starve the Parisian mob into submission. Each year afterwards, the veterans of the Commune would meet for an annual banquet in Paris to celebrate not only their amazing survival but also their revolt against the monarchists and their bourgeois supporters. The last surviving 'communard' pictured here had lived through the famine and the subsequent bloodbath in which 20–30,000 men and women were shot in the streets and their leaders executed or transported.

A Musical Memory

Louise Loring, who lived nearby in Vevey, was a contemporary of another famous singer, Mary Garden. She had been a pupil of Emma Nevada who, in turn, had sung frequently in Spain and was much admired by the Queen of Spain for her singing of Amina in Bellini's opera *La Sonnambula*.

When my husband and I arrived for dinner and were greeted by Louise, we both remarked on the splendid diamond and pearl pin she was wearing. On closer inspection, at her request, we realized it said 'Sonnambula', surmounted by an eight-pointed coronet, and was inscribed on the back –

A la eminente artista Emma Nevada
El Conde Michelena,
Madrid 6th December, 1888

There were about eighteen guests at dinner, including our neighbours, Noël Coward, Graham Payn and Cole Lesley, and I was sitting beside Louise. Imagine my feelings when, during the course of the meal, she quietly removed the brooch from her gown and pressed it into my hand, saying she had planned to leave it to me in her will, but it would give both of us more pleasure for me to have it right away! I was giddy with excitement and don't remember another thing about the evening!

The brooch is still a favourite piece that I wear frequently and that reminds me of a very generous and interesting lady.

Governments were satisfied that the working classes were as healthy as their station required them to be, but euphoria about the condition of men like these Scottish labourers, photographed at dinner in 1900, was rudely shattered when they volunteered for Boer War service. Well over one third were rejected on physical grounds and the government began to take action to improve the national diet.

DAVID TANG

A Case of Mistaken Identity

Lord Carrington was coming to dinner. He was going to arrive in Hong Kong from London in the morning and return that same evening. Some thirteen thousand miles just for dinner – and some dinner it had to be.

He was in fact coming to Hong Kong to celebrate the establishment of a joint venture between Christie's, of which he is Chairman, and the local Swire's. But the occasion was given a charity context, no doubt to mitigate any pretentiousness.

At the command of Swire's Dame Lydia Dunn (as she then was), a few of us were face-twisted into donating a piece or two for a private auction preceding the dinner for the benefit of the evening. In return we would all become hosts for the tables. Accordingly, Hong Kong's rent-a-crowd obliged and the ballroom of the Mandarin Hotel was filled.

It was a glamorous affair. The dinner was sumptuous and the men were in black tie, while the women were dripping in jewellery like Christmas trees.

Towards the end of the dinner, and not long before Lord Carrington had to catch his flight home, Dame Lydia went round all the tables with him in order to thank all the donors and hosts. When the couple came to our table, we all stood up courteously to their toast after which Dame Lydia asked Lord Carrington, pointing at me: 'Do you know David, Peter?'

Food in the World War I trenches was bad enough, except for those officers in the better regiments who had supplies sent out from Fortnum and Mason or Harrods, or, in some cases, from the cook at home. Raymond Asquith, son of the Prime Minister, wrote home to his wife: 'I found a delicious cargo of luxuries awaiting me here – scent and morphia and marmalade and cold chicken and a really admirable ham for which Mrs Gould [the cook] deserves quite full marks.' Another member of the upper classes had a photograph of his cook about whom he wrote:

*Upon the portly frame we
   look
Of one who was our former
   Cook.
No better keeper of our Store,
Did ever enter at our door.
She knew and pandered to our
   taste,
Allowed no want and yet no
   waste;
And for some thirty years and
   more
The cares of Office here she
   bore.*

THE TOAST OF THE DAY

"LADIES AND GENTLEMEN, I HAVE THE HONOUR TO GIVE YOU THE HEALTH OF THE LADIES FORMERLY OUR SUPERIORS, NOW OUR EQUALS."

One social revolution was the much wider acceptance of ladies at table, here caricatured in Punch. *Ironically, it occurred only a few years before another social revolution which took female servants away from the middle (and even lower-middle) class homes into manufacturing industry, leaving the lady of the house to fend in the kitchen as well as to appear, unruffled, as the hostess.*

I was expecting him to deny me, as I had only met him very briefly on two or three occasions.

'Yes, of course. And how are you?' Lord Carrington replied, smiling a huge smile towards me.

I was rather chuffed and my guests round the table were visibly impressed, as they also smiled, looking as if they were vicariously known to Lord Carrington.

'And congratulations,' I continued the conversation, 'I hear Rupert is getting married.'

Rupert was the son whom I did know – and I thought such slight familiarity would cement my acquaintance with the important visitor.

'Well indeed. And thank you.' Lord Carrington acknowledged to me. And waving a half goodbye towards me and still smiling all smiles, he concluded by saying: 'And very nice seeing you again, Mr Wong.'

As all my guests and I knew my name was not Mr Wong, there were two moments of awkwardness, followed by a burst of laughter. I had definitely lost face and the only rejoinder I could summon up under the circumstances was: 'And please send my love to Krystal,' I shouted at Lord Carrington.

Needless to say, his Lordship seemed a little baffled by my remark and I distinctly heard him whisper a ministerial question to Dame Lydia, asking who was Krystal. The Dame didn't seem to know either.

MARGARET THATCHER MP

Two Memories

In the eleven years that I was Prime Minister, I was privileged to attend many marvellous dinners. However, two in particular will always stand out in my memory.

The first was the historic dinner on the occasion of the 250th anniversary of 10 Downing Street as the home of the Prime Minister, which was attended by Her Majesty the Queen and the Duke of Edinburgh. Six Prime Ministers were there: Lord Stockton (Harold Macmillan), Lord Home, Lord Wilson, Lord Callaghan, Ted Heath and myself – the only time when we all dined together.

The second was the dinner we gave to thank the Armed Forces after the Falklands had been recovered. It was a great occasion and an evening full of emotional memories.

FREDDIE TRUEMAN

Bowled Out

Many years ago I was requested by Websters Brewery of Halifax to be the guest speaker at a local football league dinner at Elland Top. This was to take place on the Saturday of a Test Match at Old Trafford. The dinner was 7.30 for 8 p.m. and I realized that, with effort, I could be there by 7.40. With a ten-minute shower and change I could be 'on parade' by 7.50.

My wife, Veronica, spoke to the organizer on her arrival and explained this, which appeared to be acceptable.

I arrived at the hotel five minutes earlier than I had hoped, after phoning my story to my newspaper and broadcasting. Veronica had a cool gin and tonic waiting and my evening wear all ready to put on.

By 7.50 we were going down to the reception room as planned, only to find the place deserted, not a soul to be seen. We then followed the sound of voices, up a stairway, and there was our party, well into the main course of their meal, all in casual wear.

Somewhat embarrassed, we made our way across the ballroom floor in full evening dress, to take our places at table, declining any starters. The gentleman on my left did not say 'Good Evening, Fred,' but opened with 'You know, I blacked out on the motorway again.' My response to this comment was indescribable – for once in my life at a total loss for words. When I recovered, I said 'Don't you think you should see a doctor?' He replied 'I did, and he told me that if it should happen again I must have a specialist report and must stop driving.' (A prescription with which he appeared to disagree entirely.)

After quite some time there was no sign of any wine being offered, whereupon my wife made a tentative suggestion to the gentleman on her right, who had not given any thought to the matter. Nevertheless he arranged it. Gaining confidence on having succeeded in this venture, he took my wife to one side, asking 'How long does your husband's speech last?' 'Oh, about thirty-five minutes,' she replied. 'Oooh!' he said with a crestfallen expression, 'do you think he could cut it down to ten minutes as, really, we are here to enjoy ourselves!'

I duly obliged, the tables were removed at lightning speed, an organ was produced from behind a curtain and the assembled party happily threw themselves into sequence dancing.

We made a quiet exit, were not missed, and, still in evening dress, went to visit friends who lived round the corner from the hotel and had a good laugh at our expense.

The civilized custom of dining helps to keep men sane under adverse conditions, such as when Shackleton's Imperial Trans-Antarctic Expedition (1914–17) was trapped in the ice for months on end. Their ship, ironically named Endurance, *eventually sank – but not before the crew had held this celebratory Midwinter's Day dinner in the quarters they dubbed 'The Ritz'. The menu consisted of roast pork, peas, plum pudding and cocoa.*

SIR PETER USTINOV

Sweets For Dessert

My memories of wartime have a good deal to do with food, or rather the shortage of it, and the boring nature of most of what was available. As a result, some rather ordinary comestibles acquired a temporary glamour. In the army I spent some time at a curious establishment which also housed a number of 'boffins' – civilians with an academic background – and I vividly recall being asked to dinner by one of these professional types.

Many of my friends were surprised by this invitation, since my host had a reputation for stinginess, and had apparently never extended his hospitality to any of his colleagues. Accompanying the dinner was water, not of the greatest vintage. It was old lecturer's water, with tiny gondolas of dust clearly visible to the naked eye. The sight and taste of this unexpected nectar has absolutely effaced from my memory the meal itself, although I do remember that it was not even tempting by regimental standards.

After dinner, I was tactless enough to offer my host a Havana cigar. My father had brought some from Portugal, and they were a little powerful for me at the time. He regarded it with incredulity, almost as though I had stabbed him in the back. He didn't trust my offer; he made a gesture to take it, then withdrew his hand, and searched my face.

'Oh, no . . . may I really . . . no, indeed I shouldn't . . . what? I can't believe it. No, it's your last. No. D'you really mean it?' His hand trembled a little as he lit it, and allowed the half-forgotten vapours of untroubled civilization to invade his oral cavities. His eyes closed in ecstasy. Then he suddenly woke out of his voluptuous daydream as though some urgent social necessity were claiming his attention. He looked furtively round his room in order to find some riposte to this normal generosity which had so scurrilously invaded the stagnancy of his instincts. Suddenly he brightened.

'I tell you what . . .' he cried, and rushed to a drawer of his desk. 'Barley-sugar!'

He produced a paper bag in which some barley-sugar had been hibernating. It had by now congealed into a tortuous mass, which clung to the interior of the paper bag, and threatened to rip it to pieces if attacked in its lair.

I struggled for a while with the contents of the proffered bag, while he tried to hold it as still as possible. As the unequal struggle grew embarrassing, he was evidently suffering a frightful indecision, as though his avarice was being to put to some unusual and terrible test. At last the bubble of his thoughts burst.

'Oh never mind,' he blurted recklessly. 'Take two bits.'

KEITH WATERHOUSE

Why Lunches are more memorable than Dinners

Dinner, however enjoyable, lacks a certain spicy something – that faint but distinct air of foreignness that always hangs over lunch, bringing with it the heady tang of forbidden fruits. There is something ever so slightly wicked about even the most innocent lunch – a feeling of self-indulgence, of stolen moments, of lotus-eating. Even Sunday lunch, over which one is surely entitled to linger after a hard week's work, is accompanied by a pleasurably guilty awareness that one could be more healthily, if not more happily, occupied.

Dine, and you are unwinding after the day's labours. Lunch, and you are playing truant.

Lunch may be mildly – or intensely – illicit ('You do not,' counselled that congenial lunch companion, restaurant critic and man of letters Christopher Matthew, 'take your wife out to lunch.') Dinner, except when indulged in by out-of-town businessmen, rarely so – the affair that has reached the dining-out stage has gone far beyond the flirtatious parameters of lunch and is heading for the divorce courts.

You most decidedly do take your wife to dinner – there would be trouble if you did not – together with two other couples you owe a meal to. Reciprocation and obligation hang heavy in the air like garlic. At least one of the party will turn up late and half-cut ('Peter's going to catch up with us at the restaurant as soon as he can get away') and one of the couples will be plainly suppressing an ongoing domestic row. The bill will be staggering – there are always more guests at dinner than at lunch, they drink more and eat more, and anyway dinner costs more. You will awake with a hangover.

Admittedly, dinner at its best can be a very jolly occasion, but jolliness of that particular order and at that number of decibels is not really a characteristic of lunch, unless it is a special occasion.

Domestic help did not vanish from the grander households, as this painting shows, with permanent staff (in uniform) aided by help from the village (no uniform). In more and more homes, however, as the twentieth century progressed, the tendency developed for families to eat some of their meals in the kitchen itself, rather than the dining-room.

The nearest approximation to lunch in the evening is the romantic candlelit dinner for two, where both parties are single and as fancy-free as maybe. But here again there is an important distinction. Dinner, in these circumstances, tends to lead to bed – lunch not necessarily so. You do not (except by long-standing arrangement) as a rule offer to escort a girl home after lunch. Both or either of you may have things to do, offices to go back to, appointments to keep, a birthday card to buy. You have options to keep open or not as you choose, unlike the dinner companion who can hardly claim to be going off to pick up the dry-cleaning at getting on for midnight.

So where dinner is a commitment, lunch retains an elusiveness all its own. It is a shadow play – the delicious hint of a promise, perhaps, but not a pledge.

AUBERON WAUGH

The Wine which Whispers

For many years I have claimed as my cousin the Master of Wine, Harry Waugh, generally acknowledged as the greatest English expert on the wines of Bordeaux. I am not sure whether we are really related but it is nice to think so.

On his eightieth birthday he asked me to a small dinner party given for him by Mr Mark Birley at Mark's Club, in Charles Street, Mayfair. The food was excellent, the company delightful, but what made it most memorable for me was that we opened one of the few surviving magnums of the 1947 Château Cheval Blanc, a legendary wine about which people still talk in whispers. For many years I had been writing about wine, and sometimes felt the temptation to wonder whether or not it was all a confidence trick: that you can now buy such good wine from the New World that talk of the great Bordeaux was really nothing but snobbery and affectation. This wine convinced me for once and for all that there *is* a pot of gold at the end of the rainbow; wine writing is not all pseudery and, for those ready to open their minds to the possibility, there is a taste of the sublime waiting for those who try hard enough.

BERNARD WEATHERILL MP

A Speaker's Recollection

In 1985 I received a visit at the House of Commons from the Speaker of the Hungarian Parliament and, in the ante-room before going into dinner, I introduced her to Mr Neil Kinnock, with the words 'Madame Speaker, may I introduce you to the Leader of Her Majesty's Official Opposition?' Someone who was present, threw in for good measure 'and he is paid you know.'

At the dinner-table, in her reply to my speech of welcome, she commented; 'Mr Speaker, in my country we have a great deal of opposition, but we do not allow them to have official spokesmen – and it will be a very long time before we pay them!'

Recently I have accepted an invitation from the Speaker of the democratically elected Hungarian Parliament – could there be a more dramatic illustration of the momentous changes that have taken place in Eastern Europe within the last five years?

VICTORIA WOOD

A Sticky Business

My most memorable but least enjoyable dinner ended with my husband and myself ordering meringues glacées, which we love, and getting marrons glacés, which we loathe. Being too embarrassed to send them back, I had to smuggle them out in my handbag.

There was a sick man of Tobago
Liv'd long on rice-gruel and sago;
  But at last, to his bliss,
  The physician said this—
" To a roast leg of mutton you
    may go."

An illustration from an English book called Anecdotes and Adventures of Fifteen Gentlemen, *published in London in about 1823 captures the gleeful spirit of a midnight feast. This Tobagan gentleman has been dieting from medical necessity, but dieting as an obsession did not long post-date this illustration. Indeed, in the early 1860s, there was a fad for what was called 'banting' – reducing superfluous fat by adopting a particular diet promoted by William Banting, a London cabinet-maker who had once been very fat. Dieting today is big business, and has become a widespread preoccupation of almost all diners.*

LORD WESTBURY

A Note in the Right Direction

I remember my mother telling me this story about the late Mrs Ronald Greville who, when giving dinner parties, kept her staff up to the mark with a constant barrage of advice and, sometimes, criticism.

Her method of doing this was to keep a small pad by the side of her place with an even smaller silver pencil, with which she would write them notes such as 'Sprouts could be hotter' or 'Hurry up with the soup' or simply 'More wine'.

At one celebrated dinner she noticed that the man she had recently hired to buttle was much the worse for drink. He got more and more unsteady on his feet as the meal progressed. The hostess finally decided that his conduct had gone too far. She wrote 'You are drunk, leave the room immediately', folded up the note and called the man over and placed it on his salver. He retired politely to a corner of the room, put on his glasses and carefully read the note. Then he folded it again, placed it back on the tray, and slowly walked across the room to the far end of the table. He paused by a seat occupied by an eminent ambassador and deferentially offered him the salver and the note.

Vita Sackville-West chatting to Lord Darling at the Poetry Society's Birthday Dinner at the Café Royal in 1930, attended by descendants of the all-time poetical greats. The illustrious poetess was invited because one of her ancestors had written the earliest English drama in blank verse. Vita's left-hand neighbour seems to have given up the struggle for her attention.

VISCOUNT WEYMOUTH

An Embarrassing Dinner

It often happens, as on one particular evening, that the misunderstanding of a particular foreign phrase gives rise to some embarrassment. This was an episode which occurred in the full flush of self-conscious youth – when I was just twenty-one, during the summer of 1953, while I was living in Paris and trying to attain a standard in French which would enable me to con-

verse freely. Each morning I was attending the lectures for the *Cours de Civilisation Française* at the Sorbonne, Marcel Proust being one of the authors that we were required to study. And our lecturer was making a big point in explaining Proust's personality by proclaiming him to be *'un inverti'*.

Now in my incipient understanding of their language, I assumed that I was being told that Proust was introverted – without appreciating that there was little distinction to be drawn (in French) between being an invert, and being a pervert. It was in ignorance of such potential confusion that I turned up – fresh-faced to a degree that might be regarded as androgynous – at a dinner-party for a Parisian ball, where my dinner hostess was an English lady whom I had never previously met, and where the other guests were mostly French. Anyway I was doing my best to contend with the problems of conversing in that language, while proclaiming the distinctions (as I surmised they might be) between the Anglo-Saxon character and its Latin counterpart. I asserted (dubiously perhaps, and certainly without furnishing in myself such a good example of this superficial generalization as I appeared to suppose) that the British are introverted. But of course I was using this word *inverti*, which I had just appended to my French vocabulary. So what I was in fact telling them was that I myself was homosexual – like all the rest of my countrymen.

I should mention, parenthetically, that I had reached a stage in the evening when I had drunk as much wine as might be good for me, and (at such times) I become loquacious. But it was one of those conversations which had begun privately enough, while I endeavoured to entertain the girl sitting next to me with some degree of sincerity and conviction in my argument. I did note, however, that there was something in her expression which could only indicate that my point wasn't well taken. With too much haste, I assumed that she hadn't managed to comprehend the train of my thought. So I returned to my

The Vintners' Company's Swan Feast is still held each November. A procession composed of six musicians, two Swan Uppers with crooks, a chef bearing a stuffed swan, a Swan Marker, Beadle and Stavesman, is led into the Livery Hall by the Swan Warden. The Swan Warden presents the swan to the Master 'for the delectation of his guests.' The procession then leaves the Livery Hall and the Feast is resumed.

When the war broke out in 1939, the government had not forgotten the lessons of World War I, and ration books had been printed well in advance. Churchill himself did not bother too much about rationing, despite being issued with a ration book in democratic fashion. The story goes that one day he asked to see a typical rationed meal. When he had sampled the chop, followed by a portion of cheese and a chocolate bar, he remarked that it was not bad for a light lunch. 'But that is one week's ration, Prime Minister,' the shocked officials advised him.

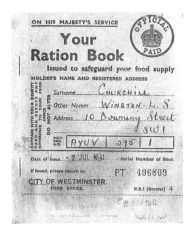

Postwar, luxurious eating returned, for those who could afford it, on a grander scale than ever before. Here the Greek shipowner Aristotle Onassis holds a party on one of his big oil tankers in the bay at Jeddah, Saudi Arabia. The passion for holding enormous parties at unusual sites has not diminished since the days of Belshazzar. The Shah of Persia held one in the desert and American millionaires have chosen equally striking venues.

theme with augmented vigour, asking others at the table to agree that I was *un inverti*, and that most of my countrymen could be regarded in the same light.

I have often found that Frenchmen believe that sexual deviation is more popular within British culture than within French – something to do with their conviction that Englishmen are driven to homosexuality by the segregated eccentricity of our public school educational system. So no one expressed any surprise that I should be taking this line of argument. Indeed they were treating me with an amused blend of sympathy and surprise that I should be making such a song and dance about the whole business. There was one who unsuccessfully endeavoured to conceal a smile behind a hand raised pensively to the chin, and another who was nodding his head gravely and telling me that my point had been understood. But I could see from his expression that he didn't regard himself as my ally. And my English hostess was glaring at me reprovingly, as if I was somehow letting down the side.

I failed to fathom, on that particular evening, how it was that my conversation appeared to be intriguing the whole company, without any of them actually coming out in my support. And the more I persevered with the discussion, the more I was sinking into a mire of confusion. The moment arrived when my hostess quite firmly changed the subject. While it took me some weeks to comprehend the gaucherie of my performance, such understanding did eventually dawn once my misuse of the French language had been explained to me. No opportunities for reparation were then open to me, however. And I never did get invited to grace this lady's table on any subsequent occasion.

ALAN WHICKER

A Festive Occasion

Almost forty years ago, I found myself in the middle of a few ugly Middle Eastern scenes reminiscent of the recent Gulf war – though with different friends and enemies. The Egyptian Wafd party was struggling to drive us out of their kingdom; the British Army had withdrawn its 80,000 men from the Nile Delta into the defended Canal Zone base, and terrorism and baying for British blood continued.

From the Semiramis Hotel in Cairo I set out for the Zone in a decrepit taxi; the road from Ismailia to Army Headquarters at Moascar ran alongside a foul turgid moat called, as you might expect, the Sweet Water Canal. It contained dead dogs and old bicycles and was used for drinking and bathing; its banks were also the local lavatory. Egyptian snipers within the Casbah would fire across at military transport using the road, which in despatches we learned to call – as you also might expect – Murder Mile. Another popular might-expect phrase at the time, I remember, was 'Death from the bougainvillaea'.

Terrorism had become insupportable, so the Army was reacting; I urged my reluctant driver to follow the Centurion tanks into Ismailia. Their twenty-pounders blew a few chunks off the Egyptian police headquarters where the attacks were being organized, killing 46 and wounding 60. After a noisy morning, the revolutionary ardour cooled, and for a while afterwards fewer British soldiers were ambushed and murdered.

The position of the Press during this emergency was unusual: we were not War Correspondents because there was no war. That's reasonable. The catch was that, as unaccredited civilians, we could not be offered WD accommodation or transport. However since we were patently not Egyptian, and seemed to be more or less on the Army's side . . . they were at least prepared to defend us – during normal working hours, of course.

As Christmas approached, they decided to move us out of sight and mind into the local United Services Club; this stood outside the guarded perimeter, so was unused and deserted. Some twenty members of the international Press – British and American, with a leavening of French, Belgians and Swiss – were formally escorted there by armoured cars, for the Christmas holiday. This *could* have been for our protection, to make sure the War Department had no innocent blood on its hands.

Having assured themselves that the Club's storeroom contained an adequate supply of tinned NAAFI sausages and some brown sauce for our Christmas dinner, the Army retreated with many expressions of seasonal goodwill to enjoy its own holiday in comfortable homes behind barricades, leaving us to face whatever the terrorists might have in mind.

We locked the doors. We were unarmed, so attack was not the best form of defence. We opened the sausages without much festive joy, and got ready to repel boarders. It was a holiday celebration that had no significance at all for the hostile Egyptians lurking outside and, under those particular circumstances, not much for us.

Since we had no transport and no communications, there was no work. Portable typewriters remained closed. Dejected, we resigned ourselves to the recreational facility available: one dart-

Painters no longer had the urge to paint dinners, or perhaps it was that their patrons no longer felt the urge to put twentieth-century food on the canvas. Certainly the Impressionists and their successors preferred the landscape, the still life or the human figure. This picture of a dinner by lamplight, painted by Felix Vallotton (1865–1925) is an exception.

board. Fortunately the bar shelves were weighed down with spirits and Star beer, so the first game of the season began with ascending merriment.

Then from the silent night outside, a fusillade of rifle fire shattered all the windows – and much of our stock of good cheer. It seemed a poor start to the festivities.

Some correspondents were cut by flying glass, but no one was hit. We lay on the floor in the dark, reflecting upon Goodwill to All Men. When the shouting died down, Jacques Marcuse, from Agence France Presse, thoughtfully spread cups around to collect dripping cognac. Then we put out the remaining lights and made a careful inspection.

It seemed our floodlit dartboard was in a direct line of fire from the top of the minaret above the Ismailia mosque; our unfriendly neighbourhood snipers across the canal had it firmly in their telescopic sights.

They evidently assumed we were some new and threatening military outpost, and were taking steps. It was only by the grace of Allah, and an inborn and God-given luck of marksmanship, that they failed to double-top us. This was *Christmas*?

Dismissing the idea of a white flag as asking for trouble, we gave them First Fall, deserted our bullet-ridden dartboard and retreated to the lounge at the back for those NAAFI sausages, washed down by beer from broken bottles. It was a memorable meal, unfortunately.

Then followed the entertainment: an intense poker game that went on for three days and nights. If Father Christmas had come down the air conditioning, we would not have noticed – unless he wanted to ante-up and take a hand.

Three days later we were rescued by troops in armoured cars, who had all had a *great* Christmas dinner, thank you very much. . . .

MICHAEL WINNER

Chopsticks

I still come out in a cold sweat when I recall the dinner party I organized to follow the première of my film *Death Wish*.

One hundred guests were to leave the cinema in Leicester Square at 10.30 p.m., dive into their cars and head for my house in Holland Park.

My usual caterer had gone out of business (probably because of the discounts I always demanded!) and I had been persuaded by Peter, the charming manager of my local Chinese restaurant, that he and his merry men would organize the most wonderful and imaginative Chinese dinner.

I arrived home from the première, leaving my friends to watch the film, at around 9.30 p.m. Peter had decorated my house with a large number of menus, advertising signs, and cards for his restaurant. There was no sign of food, which I was assured would arrive, together with fifteen waiters and three chefs, at 10 o'clock.

I suggested all the advertising material should be removed at once. Peter took it away and went back to the restaurant to organize things.

At 10 o'clock there was no sign of anybody turning up with the food. At ten past ten there was no sign of it either. I telephoned the restaurant, which they had not closed for the evening, and was told they were very busy but would be coming shortly.

By 10.30, with the guests only some twenty minutes away, there was still no sign of anyone at all! Every time I rang the restaurant a rather snappy voice said 'We'll be there' and put the phone down on me!

I was, to put it mildly, beginning to get nervous. Desperately, I knelt down to look out of one of the few low windows from which I could see the roadway through the trees, praying that any passing car would stop and disgorge a large number of Chinese gentlemen carrying food. My Irish housekeeper, in a complete panic, walked up and down muttering that there were only eggs and toast in the kitchen. Should she start to prepare them?

At ten to eleven, with the housekeeper and I still the only people in the house, a car pulled up and stopped. At last, I thought, the caterers!

But no! It was the first of the guests! They swung up the garden path, laughing and chatting and walked cheerfully into the house. I was by now sweating profusely, shaking, and wondering how I could explain to one hundred guests that not a morsel of food was available to eat unless they wanted to share a few slices of toast and six eggs!

There was no one to help me pour the drinks, so I had a go myself, as other guests swarmed in, hungry, after their evening at the movies.

'I hope you like toast and eggs,' I said nervously. My guests laughed. What a joker he is, they thought to themselves.

Film stars, newspaper editors, TV celebrities – all kept arriving. The room was now filling with fifty people. Drinks were slowly served by me! Still no sign of any food, waiters, or anything else at all!

'Boiled cod, sir? For *you*, sir?'

As artists gave up, so cartoonists took on the task of presenting trenchermen and women at work. These examples are by Nicolas Bentley and Osbert Lancaster, typical of the 1930s and 1950s respectively. Nancy Mitford had written a famous article explaining that eating peas off the knife was non-U (i.e. not acceptable). Maudie Littlehampton disagrees.

"Oh, to hell with Nancy Mitford! What I always say is — if it's ME it's U!" 1.5.56

At ten minutes past eleven, with guests thick on the front path walking toward my door, I looked out to see the visitors thrust aside as an army of Chinese gentlemen pushed through, knocking them hither and thither as they carried in heavy boxes of food and delicacies.

I have to say from then on it was a quick recovery! Somehow or other, quite shortly thereafter, immaculate waiters were handing round hot Chinese canapés, and no one but I seemed to be taking the delay very seriously.

You may wonder why, in view of such a nerve-racking experience, I chose the same group to cater for my next première, *The Wicked Lady.*

This time I was adamant they should make up for the somewhat eccentric performance the year before. I insisted that every single member of the staff plus all the food were in the house at half-past eight and were never to leave it. And indeed they were: waiters, chefs, and the owner of the company.

When Faye Dunaway and I came back from the première, leaving the guests watching the film, we sat and had a splendid dinner with twenty waiters to serve it.

I felt completely secure.

At twenty to eleven the doorbell rang. It was the first of the guests. I poked my head into the kitchen, knowing that everybody was there and all would be in order. What greeted me was some twenty Chinese chaps deep in conversation, some playing cards, others smoking, all having a hell of a time, with none of the food unwrapped and none of the bottles opened!

However, this time recovery was even speedier, and everything went off extremely well.

I've only had four large dinner parties in my house in the thirty years i have lived in it. Not surprising really, is it?

GOOGIE WITHERS

Back-Stage Memories

Many years ago, we all used to go to the Ivy restaurant and later to the Caprice: one felt nothing but admiration and respect for Mario Galati, owner of both of them. The Ivy was very much *the* theatre place to go to, and to be *seen in*, and Mario looked after us all wonderfully well, even in the war with those five-bob meals! When we moved to the Caprice, we discovered something else about him. On Sundays (his only day off – otherwise getting up at 4.00 a.m. daily to go to the markets, and at every meal throughout the week), he gave a meal at his house which he cooked himself and to which he invited various people who had been long-standing clients of his.

It was a considerable honour, believe me, and John and I were very lucky to have gone to one of them. We drove somewhere north west – I think bordering Hampstead/Golders Green, as far as I can remember – to a suburban house. Once past the front door, we walked straight into Italy. As it was a lovely summer's evening we dined on a terrace at the back covered with a vine, with the grapes hanging down in huge bunches – very sour sadly. However, the meal, completely Italian, with beautiful pasta, was cooked by Mario and went on for what seemed hours, helped along by very many bottles of Chianti and Verdicchio. Afterwards Mario played and sang Neapolitan songs on his guitar. We also met his wife for the first time (she was like the woman who played Marlon Brando's wife in *The Godfather*) and his daughter Mary, who became a writer of note.

There is one more thing to add to this story. Mario saw to it that if an actor or actress was a bit broke and out of work at any time, he gave them supper at the Caprice with wine, once a week, on the house. A very nice man.

SIR HUGH WONTNER

Lèse-majesté

When I was Lord Mayor of London in 1974, Her Majesty Queen Elizabeth the Queen Mother graciously attended a private dinner party given by myself and the Lady Mayoress.

I had previously enquired of Queen Elizabeth whether Her Majesty had ever been shown the cells beneath the Mansion House Court, where many notable people had awaited their trial. As Her Majesty replied that she had never seen these cells, after dinner I conducted Queen Elizabeth to that part of the building used for the detention of people summoned to appear in Court, and there showed Her Majesty the cell in which Mrs Pankhurst, the celebrated suffragette, had once been held.

After looking at this and other cells, Her Majesty ascended a handy staircase nearby – with a view to returning to the body of the Mansion House. Unfortunately this staircase led directly to the dock. As the staircase was rather narrow and Her Majesty was wearing a crinoline skirt, I was unable to deter her.

To the astonishment of the Recorder of London (another guest at the dinner) who happened to be sitting on the Bench in the Chief Magistrate's seat, the Queen Mother suddenly appeared in the dock, an experience that Her Majesty subsequently admitted she had never had before.

ERNIE WISE

Memorable for Others

When I joined the Merchant Marine in World War II, I was trained as a steward. 'From show business to this!' I mused, surveying an endlessly mournful scene. I was trained to wait on tables, trained to set tables, trained to clear tables, trained to lift them, shift them, stack them and, probably, if I had stayed long enough, to dance on them as well. I wasn't taught to cook.

My first posting, once trained, was as a cook. I boarded a ship called *The Firelighter* and found myself in charge of the

In the world at large, there are still many millions who have not succumbed to western dining habits, as well as millions more whose dinners fail to provide adequate nourishment. Typical of the former are the Tongans, who eat with their fingers food which is laid before them on stretchers rather than on tables and plates. This photograph was taken in 1953 when the Queen and the Duke of Edinburgh visited the Pacific island to meet again Queen Salote, who had been a guest at the Queen's coronation.

The shape of things to come? American astronauts aboard the space shuttle Atlantis *make the most of their diet of freeze-dried, pre-packaged food. No need for weight-watching here.*

well-being of the engineers. There was a Chief Engineer, a First and Second Engineer and what they called the Donkey Man who did everything the first three couldn't or wouldn't do.

You can imagine what sort of havoc an inexperienced eighteen-year-old can wreak in the kitchen, or galley as I learnt to call it, when he is first put in charge of a cooking range the size of a small warehouse. After a few days I had mastered the art of preparing soup. Get a bag of bones from somewhere – ask no questions about precisely where – tip them into a saucepan full of water, boil them for a few minutes then add vegetables. Serve, without salt, while the vegetables are still hard and wait for the engineers' compliments.

No compliments came, of course, but nor did complaints. They ate it all without a grumble. The same thing happened when I overcooked the meat and undercooked the potatoes. They ate everything I put before them as if I were a chef on temporary loan from the Ritz. This I took to be a measure of how rough life was going to be at sea. If they could stomach this sort of cooking, I reasoned, what sort of grub had they been getting before?

The food, as things turned out, was the least of their worries. Though the Merchant Navy didn't have the glamorous image of its Royal counterpart, it was suffering fantastic casualties performing its part in the war effort. Ferrying essential supplies to the capital, it was the constant target of air and sea attack, and on my particular run an awful lot of people, especially Tynesiders, lost their lives.

The House of Hine

In an era when standardization and world-embracing brands have made the pursuit of individuality and excellence something of an endangered species, the two-hundred-year-old firm of Thomas Hine has succeeded in remaining true to its traditions of excellence. To achieve this objective, the present generation of the family – Bernard and Jacques Hine – have been fortunate in finding a secure haven within the LVMH group, where the even older traditions of Ruinart have flourished alongside the market leader, Moet & Chandon. Here the philosophy of excellence is well understood and respected.

The story of Hine begins in Dorset. In common with neighbouring Somerset, it had asserted its independence of mind in the seventeenth century, with a strong dose of puritanism. By the eighteenth century, this had become solid nonconformity, and nonconformists, barred by law from entering the professions or holding a commission in the army or navy, had become the traders and businessmen who were the backbone of the Industrial Revolution. This was Thomas Hine's background.

Born in Beaminster, on the Somerset border, in 1775, his family seem to have had trading links with France, although we cannot be sure of their nature. All we do know is that, as the frenzy of the French Revolution began to run out of control, the young Thomas set out for Jarnac to perfect his French.

That the choice should have fallen on Jarnac is unlikely to have been by chance. Many Englishmen, Scotsmen and Irishmen were trading and settling in Aquitaine in the eighteenth century, most in and around Bordeaux – but, at the same time, the Cognac trade had begun to be developed, mainly by men from these islands. As it was, the sixteen-year-old Thomas had no sooner arrived than he found himself incarcerated in the Château de Jarnac, all subjects of King George III having been declared 'enemies of the People'. Fortunately, calmer times soon prevailed. Thomas stayed on in Jarnac, married Françoise Elisabeth from an old Cognac family in 1797 and, with this union, also married into the Cognac business. In the following year, Thomas Georges Hine was born and the dynasty was launched.

At this point, we might pause to recall that it had been the Dutch who had begun by distilling the poor acid white wines of the Charente, before

Thomas Hine & Co., Quai de l'Orangerie, Jarnac.

At work in their tasting room: Jacques and Bernard Hine.

shipping them home – where they were drunk diluted with water. This process both made them stable and reduced their volume. The resulting 'burnt wines', or brandewijn, became known in English as brandy. It was then in the eighteenth century that enterprising merchants, mostly from the British Isles, began to improve their brandies by ageing them in Limousin oak casks, and the miracle of Cognac, as we know it, was born.

The Hines played an important part in the development of Cognac in the nineteenth century. In 1860, a French geologist called Coquand visited the region in the company of a professional taster of wine and brandy. While one analysed the soil, the other tasted the brandies. When they compared their results, Coquand found that they vindicated his theory that there was a direct relationship between the soil and the quality of the Cognacs they produced. As in Champagne, it was found that the limestone soils of the Grande Champagne and the Petite Champagne produced the finest Cognacs, and so it was that Hine began to concentrate on producing Cognacs from this, the heart of the region, for their finest Vintage Brandies. And, at about the same time, Hine began shipping their Cognacs in bottle instead of in cask, with the sole exception of their famous Early Landed Cognacs.

Today, Bernard and Jacques Hine represent the sixth generation of the family who have worked in the business. The world is a very different one, but the ideals and principles which guide the business have remained remarkably constant. Their fathers, the brothers François and Robert, had been faced with the problems of rebuilding the business after the Second World War. To the cousins Bernard and Jacques, both born in 1939, fell the task of adapting to the new commercial realities of the World Market. Realizing that they could not hope to compete with the big brigades in the mass market of three-star Cognac, they set their sights on what Hine had always done best, and determined to go for quality.

The virtues of clear objectives and lucid vision have brought their rewards. In 1962, Hine became the only Cognac to receive the Royal Warrant from Queen Elizabeth II, the ultimate seal of distinction on the British Market. Then, during the years after 1960, when the bottling of Vintage Cognac in France was stopped, they kept alive this ultimate expression of individuality in Cognac by exporting a few of their finest casks of two and three-year-old Grande Champagne Cognacs for ageing under Customs supervision in the UK. Furthermore, they now have their own cellars in Bristol to mature these

Early Landed beauties under their own control. They have led the way in collaborating with the French authorities in instituting a new regime which will revive the possibility, once more, of ageing and bottling Vintage Cognacs in the land of their birth.

The demand for high quality Fine and Grande Champagne Cognacs cannot, of course, be met simply by such delectable rarities as Vintage Cognac, any more than the demand for Champagne can be met by the Vintage variety. So Hine has concentrated its efforts on building up stocks to provide regular supplies of the very finest old mature Cognacs, blended to a consistent quality and style.

It is appropriate that the pinnacle of the blending art of Bernard and Jacques Hine should be called Family Reserve. The aim here is not to produce an unchanging blend, as with their magnificent Triomphe, but to create something of distinct individuality at the very highest level from among their oldest vintage reserves. For the lover of vintage Cognac, this is the nearest approach in terms of its delicate fruit, its accent on liveliness rather than richness, the delicacy that only comes from the long ageing, for forty years or more, of the finest Grande Champagne Cognac.

As I sat in the salon of the old house on the Quai de l'Orangerie, nosing a glass of Family Reserve in the company of Bernard and Jacques, I studied the portraits of the 15 members of the family on the label, from Thomas Hine to my hosts. I felt that, if the shades of their forebears were looking down on us, they would not be displeased, and would still have felt comfortable in that reassuring room, looking out on the Charente.

David Peppercorn
Master of Wine

The Order of St John

The Order of St John was originally founded almost 1000 years ago to care for pilgrims visiting Jerusalem and its history in London dates back to 1144 with the Priory in Clerkenwell. From this Order developed two charitable foundations: the St John Opthalmic Hospital in Jerusalem and St John Ambulance. These two organizations have their respective fields of work, but both uphold the St John motto 'For the Service of Mankind' in everything they do.

First opened in 1882, the St John Opthalmic Hospital in Jerusalem is one of the busiest eye hospitals in the world. Its present building houses 80 beds and is manned by a staff of international surgeons and nurses. Over 50,000 patients are treated every year regardless of race, creed or ability to pay. Those unable to travel to the Hospital are served by the Outreach team who make regular visits to outlying villages to perform simple sight-saving operations and give all-important eye-tests.

St John Ambulance was formed in 1877 for the instruction of First Aid, nursing and hygiene. Ensuring that as many members of the public as possible possess basic life-saving skills remains a primary aim of the organization today. Should you be unfortunate enough to be involved in an accident, you may have to depend on the first passer-by to administer life-saving treatment. St John issues over 200,000 certificates every year to members of the public who successfully master these skills and is the leading First Aid training organization used by industry and commerce.

Children also train with St John. The St John Ambulance 'Three Cross Award' video teaching programme can be incorporated into the school curriculum and many children have already used their First Aid knowledge to treat parents and schoolfriends. From as young as six, children are able to become active members of St John Ambulance. The Badgers, launched in 1987, follow the 'Badger Course in Absolutely Everything' and take part in a wide variety of fun-based activities in addition to learning First Aid.

St John Cadets play a more active role within the Brigade, assisting adult members with public duties and developing their First Aid, Caring and Nursing skills. Outdoor pursuits and trying new activities are a natural part of Cadet life – from taking part in the Duke of Edinburgh's Award Scheme to mastering the computer or learning to canoe. Through the Links Scheme Cadets are encouraged to continue their involvement with St John once they enter higher education, whilst people wishing to work with the youth of St John can follow the Youth Leader Training package.

Brigade members give over four million hours of their time every year to work in the community and attend First Aid duties. Over 80 per cent of public events have First Aid cover provided by St John Ambulance volunteers, but St John does not restrict its activities to the ground. The Air Wing is a twenty-four hour service marshalling volunteer pilots and aircraft to fly donor organs and teams throughout Europe. The Aeromedical Service, working in conjunction with the Automobile Association, supplies fully qualified doctors and nurses to assist in flying home the sick and injured from anywhere in the world.

Look around you and someone nearby will have been trained by St John or have benefited from treatment by a St John member. Since those first Hospitallers 1000 years ago, St John Ambulance has been serving mankind and the organization is as committed today as it was then.

List of Contributors

Joss Ackland	11	James Galway	57	Countess Mountbatten of		
Sir Harold Acton	11	Bob Geldof	58	Burma		108
Lord Alexander of Weedon	12	Sir John Gielgud	59			
Sir Hardy Amies	13	Sir Nicholas Goodison	60	Eric Newby		115
Evelyn Anthony	14	Lord Goodman	60			
Jeffrey Archer	16	Lord Grade of Elstree	61	Lord Palumbo of		
		Lucinda Green	62	Walbrook		111
Christabel Bielenburg	16			Michael Parkinson		113
Colonel John		Sir John Harvey-Jones	63	Matthew Parris		113
Blashford-Snell	18	Max Hastings	64	The Hon. Andrew		
Rabbi Lionel Blue	20	Denis Healey MP	64	Peacock MP		114
Dirk Bogarde	22	Edward Heath MP	65	Lester Piggott		114
Chris Bonington	22	Major Dick Hern	65	Libby Purves		115
Richard Briers	24	James Herriot	67			
Michael Broadbent	25	Don Hewitson	69	Esther Rantzen		115
Anthony Burgess	26	David Hicks	69	The Hon. Sir Denys		
		Frankie Howerd	70	Roberts		117
Lord Carrington	27	Barry Humphreys	72	Jancis Robinson		122
Dame Barbara Cartland	29	Elspeth Huxley	75	Anita Roddick		128
Sir Hugh Casson	30			Jean Rook		129
Major Sir Rupert Clarke	31	Hammond Innes	77	Michel Roux		130
Joan Collins	32					
Henry Cooper	30	Nancy Jarratt	78	Richard Shepherd		133
Jilly Cooper	33	Hugh Johnson	80	Ned Sherrin		132
Alan Coren	34			Lady Soames		133
		Lord King of Wartnaby	82	Jackie Stewart		135
Sir Francis Dashwood	36			Serena Sutcliffe		136
Sir Robin Day	37	Cleo Laine	83	Dame Joan Sutherland		137
Len Deighton	38	James Lees-Milne	83			
Lord Denham	39	Prue Leith	86	David Tang		138
The Duchess of		Bernard Levin	90	Margaret Thatcher MP		139
Devonshire	42	Maureen Lipman	88	Freddie Trueman		139
Jason Donovan	43	Elizabeth Longford	89			
William Douglas-Home	44	Dame Vera Lynn	89	Sir Peter Ustinov		141
				Keith Waterhouse		142
Len Evans	45	Julia McKenzie	97	Auberon Waugh		144
		Leo McKern	95	Bernard Weatherill MP		144
Sir Nicholas Fairbairn		Spike Milligan	98	Lord Westbury		145
of Fordell	50	Roger Moate MP	100	Viscount Weymouth		145
Sir Ranulph Fiennes	52	Bob Monkhouse	100	Alan Whicker		148
Lord Forte of Ripley	52	Lord Montagu of Beaulieu	102	Michael Winner		150
Michael Frayn	48	Robert Morley	103	Ernie Wise		153
Christopher Fry	54	Jan Morris	103	Googie Withers		152
		John Mortimer	105	Sir Hugh Wontner		152
Sandy Gall	55	Anton Mosimann	107	Victoria Wood		144

Acknowledgements

Editorial Credits:

Joss Ackland *I must be in there somewhere*
(Hodder & Stoughton)
Sir Harold Acton extract from: Edward
Whitley (ed.) *The Graduate*
(Hamish Hamilton)
Christabel Bielenburg *The Past Is Myself*
(Transworld)
Rabbi Lionel Blue *Blue Heaven*
(Hodder & Stoughton)
Dirk Bogarde *Backcloth* (Viking)
Richard Briers *Natter Natter* (J. M. Dent)
Anthony Burgess *Little Wilson and Big God*
(Heinemann)
Joan Collins *Past Imperfect* (W. H. Allen)
Alan Coren *More Like Old Times*
(Robson Books)
Sir Francis Dashwood *The Dashwoods of West
Wycombe* (Aurum Press)
Sir Robin Day *Grand Inquisitor*
(Weidenfeld & Nicolson)
Len Deighton *The ABC of French Food*
(Random Century)
Michael Frayn *The Original Michael Frayn*
(Salamander Press)
Bob Geldof *Is that it?* (Sidgwick & Jackson)
Sir John Gielgud *An Actor and His Time*
(Sidgwick & Jackson)
Max Hastings *Outside Days* (Michael Joseph)
Denis Healey *The Time of My Life*
(Michael Joseph/Penguin)
Elspeth Huxley *The Flame Trees of Thika*
(Chatto & Windus)
James Lees-Milne *Another Self* (Faber & Faber)

Prue Leith *Great Dishes from the British
Gastronomic Academy* (MacDonald Orbis)
Bernard Levin *If music be the food of love, it's
just as well* (1976 Glyndebourne Festival
Programme Book)
Maureen Lipman *How Was It For You?*
(Robson Books)
Leo McKern *Just Resting* (Methuen)
Spike Milligan *It Ends with Magic*
(Michael Joseph)
Roger Moate MP: reprinted from *Kindly Sit
Down!* (Buchan & Enright)
Robert Morley *The Pleasures of Age*
(Coronet Books: Hodder & Stoughton)
Jan Morris *Pleasures of a Tangled Life*
(Barrie & Jenkins)
John Mortimer *Clinging to the Wreckage*
(Weidenfeld & Nicolson/Penguin)
Eric Newby *On the Shores of the Mediterranean*
(Collins Harvill)
Matthew Parris *Inca-Kola*
(Weidenfeld & Nicolson)
Libby Purves *One Summer's Grace*
(Grafton Books)
Jancis Robinson *Jancis Robinson's Food and
Wine Adventures* (Headline)
Mary Soames *Clementine Churchill*
(Cassell)
Sir Peter Ustinov *Dear Me* (Penguin)
Keith Waterhouse *The Theory and Practice of
Lunch* (Michael Joseph)
Ernie Wise *Still on My Way to Hollywood*
(Duckworth)

Picture Credits:

Ancient Art & Architecture Collection 13, 18, 24, 30, 34, 36, 37
Bodleian Library, Oxford 14, 28
Bridgeman Art Library 2, 9, 17, 22–23, 32, 38, 39, 40–41, 42, 43, 44, 50, 51, 56–57, 62, 63, 72, 75, 76,
78–79, 90, 93, 101, 108, 109, 112, 114, 120, 126, 131, 134, 149
The British Library 29
Christie's Colour Library 15, 19, 20, 25, 35, 45, 46, 49, 59, 60, 61, 80, 86, 87
Fine Art Photographs & Library Ltd 104, 110, 131
Folger Shakespeare Library 53
Historic Royal Palaces Agency (Photographer Earl Beesley) 47
Hulton Picture Company 27, 54, 66, 77, 82, 84, 85, 91, 95, 96, 97, 99, 106, 116, 118, 132, 136, 145, 147, 153
Imperial War Museum 138, 147
India Office Library 92
John Strickland Goodall 10
Mary Evans Picture Library 8, 12, 58, 73, 98, 100, 119, 122, 123, 130, 139
Royal Geographical Society 140
Sotheby's 21
Syndication International Library 71, 137
Telegraph Colour Library 154
The Master and Wardens of the Vintners' Company 146
Walker Art Gallery 26
Werner Forman Archive 31, 33